Getting It Right

Getting It Right

REFLECTIONS ON A LIFE
SPANNING A CENTURY

Jim McDougall

Getting It Right: Reflections on a Life Spanning a Century
Copyright © 2023 by Jim McDougall. All rights reserved.

ISBN 979-8-218-14933-8

Book Design by Paul Nylander | Illustrada Design

Front cover: Jim and Von McDougall on Jim's 90th birthday, photo by Frank Audrain.
Back cover, left to right: Jim McDougall returning from the South Pacific, p. 2; Cargill Wild West Marketing Campaign, p. 129; Jim's teaching years, p. 38; Jim with many of his grandkids and great grandkids, p. 221.

Printed in the United States of America (Second Printing)

Published by The Jim McDougall Family

This is a work of nonfiction. All names and quotes are accurate to the best of the author's knowledge.

*For Von, the love of my life,
and for my six children,
Dana, Betsy, Jayne, Jackie, Sandy and Jamie,
whom I hold dear as the
greatest treasures of my life.*

With Von. Me with our six diamonds from left to right: Jayne, Betsy, Jackie, Jamie, Dana, and Sandy.

Contents

Acknowledgments................................xi
Acknowledgments for *Getting it Right:*
 Reflections on a Life Spanning a Century . *xiii*

Foreword...xvii

Preface...xxi

Chapter One: The College Years 1
 The Days Following Discharge from the Navy 1
 Developments on My Family's Farm 6
 The Wedding and Newlywed Phase 13
 Life at Yankton College.......................19
 Life at South Dakota State University...........32

Chapter Two: The Teaching Years 37
    Interviewing for Teaching Positions 37
    My First Teaching Position in Hayes and Sulfur Springs, Iowa 39
    My Teaching Position in Kingsley, Iowa 66

Chapter Three: My Career with Cargill 69

Part One: Helping Ignite the Evolution of the Animal Feed Industry 74
    The Advent of Diethylstilbestrol : A Ground-Breaking Development in the Cattle Feed Industry 74
    Getting Hired and Starting out with Cargill 76
    Concept of the Balanced Ration 82
    Evolution in Marketing Strategies 83
    Development of Regional Feeder Meetings 89
    The Prescription Feeding Program 94
    The Cargill Feedlot System 110
    Revising Feedlot Objectives 112
    Cargill Feedlot Group 117
    Cargill Feedlot Seminar 118
    Caprock Industries 127
    Annual Cargill Marketing Meeting 127
    Key Marketing Colleagues 130

Part Two: My Involvement with Cargill's Research and Marketing Innovations 132
    The Challenge to Increase Technological Advances in the Feed Industry 132
    Cargill Nutrena's Research Farm.............. 136
    Three-Stage Sow Feeding Program 138
    Development of the Isolation Systems......... 142
    The Role of Pharmaceuticals 151
    Nutrena's Controlled Release Liquid Supplement............................... 154
    Classes for Territory Managers at the Research Farm..................................... 160
    Marketing and Salesmanship Aspects 162
    Litigation 165
    Cargill's Mission and Values.................. 168

Part Three: Industry News Articles 172

Chapter Four: Family Life 195
    My Wife Von: The Heart of our Family 195
    Our Homes in Richfield and Minnetonka, Minnesota 206
    The Six Diamonds.......................... 222
    My Health History 246

Chapter Five: Travel Memoirs 261
   Vacations and Family Trips................... 267
   Cargill Business Trips 272
   Cargill Fishing Trips 278
   Elder Hostels (Road Scholar Trips)............ 281
   Consulting Trips............................. 287
   Squadron Reunions and Honor Flight 321

Conclusion 325

About the Author 327

Acknowledgments

I feel fortunate to have had the time and the help I needed to be able to write my memoirs. The process of trying to capture my most memorable experiences in writing has helped me reflect back on a long, eventful and rewarding life. It has also helped me to share the highlights of my life experiences with my family and friends and to preserve many of my fondest memories for posterity. If there are any kernels of wisdom to be found in my memoirs, I hope my children, grandchildren, and great grandchildren will benefit from them.

First and foremost, I would like to thank my daughters, Jackie Seeman and Betsy Gibbs, for the countless hours they spent helping me to organize materials for my memoirs, conducting research on background information when needed, interviewing me to hear my stories, recording these stories both on audiotape and on paper, and working with me on the wording "to get it right" with my memoir projects. Jackie was instrumental in helping me write *Almost Famous* and *The Road to Love*, Jackie and Betsy teamed up on *Conflict to Combat in the South Pacific*, with Jackie leading the way and Betsy assisting, and finally, Betsy helped me complete the last phase of my memoirs with my final book, *Getting it Right: Reflections on a Life Spanning a Century*.

When I first started working on my memoirs, I was in my early 90's, and I started discussing my preliminary ideas

With my daughters Jackie and Betsy at the Minnesota History Museum in October 2021, where I was featured on a veterans' panel on Naval Aerial Combat in WWII.

with family members, creating timelines and outlines, and gathering documentation. Unfortunately, as I approached my late 90's, my eyesight started rapidly deteriorating, and I wasn't able to read and write very well on my own. If it had not been for Jackie and Betsy, my memoirs would never have been written, and I am deeply grateful for their assistance. Both of them have told me that they were very appreciative of the time they were able to spend working with me on these memoir projects, and I in turn treasured all the time I spent with them. Two of the books were written primarily during the Covid-19 pandemic, and working with my daughters on these projects helped me to stay engaged and productive during this otherwise isolating time.

Acknowledgments for *Getting it Right: Reflections on a Life Spanning a Century*

Thank you to my daughter, Betsy, for helping me translate my memories about my career years, family life, and travels, into written form so that they could be shared with others now and beyond my lifetime. Without her help, this portion of my memoirs would not have been completed. I deeply appreciate the incredible amount of time, energy and effort she put into helping me capture my stories in writing and complete the last chapters of my memoirs.

I would also like to sincerely thank my son, Jamie McDougall, for proofing and editing the material for

Getting it Right, and also for helping to update some of the marketing and business terminology. Thank you to my other daughters, Dana Audrain, Jayne Neal, Jackie Seeman, and Sandy LaTourelle, for reviewing the drafts and making helpful comments as well.

Thank you to my niece, Heidi Swanson Avedisian, Founder and Principal, White Ink Co., Chicago/New York, for her thoughtful editing of the final draft of this book.

Thank you to my brother Mark McDougall, who worked for Cargill for 38 years as a Territory Manager, and who, with his wife Jeanie, reviewed both earlier and later drafts of the book and provided valuable feedback.

With Betsy and my brother Mark working on *Getting it Right*.

Acknowledgments

Thank you to my entire family for helping create all the memories that I was able to share.

Thank you to Jay Reich for technical assistance with the photos in this book.

I am incredibly indebted to Cargill, Incorporated, for generously giving me permission to use selected photographs and articles from their archives.

Thank you to Jennifer Johnson, Director of Corporate Archives, Cargill, Incorporated, for her invaluable assistance in helping me to communicate with Cargill and gain access to the relevant information and photographs from the Cargill archives, and for reviewing this book in final draft form. Thank you also to Bruce Bruemmer, retired Director of Corporate Archives with Cargill, who interviewed me for the archives in 2016 and reviewed preliminary drafts of the chapters from *Getting it Right* that related to Cargill.

Finally, I'd like to thank Paul Nylander for his talent and expertise in design, typesetting, and photo processing. His creative and technical skills were just what we needed to complete this project.

Foreword

Jim was very aware of what a long, productive, and lucky life he had lived and he was always very appreciative of his blessings. He'd had a lot of close calls during his lifetime. He told me one time, for example, during World War Two at night when he was in the open bow area in the front of the PBY Catalina, that the pilot asked him to look back, so he leaned out, nearly lost his balance, and almost fell out of the plane. Fortunately for all of us, his heels caught on the opposite edge of the turret and he regained his balance in time.

Jim was always very interesting to talk to with these little details that I'd never heard before, for instance, that in a PBY they always sharpened and would carry a big handful of wooden pencils for the rough landings on the ocean. When the plane landed on the water, apparently lots of rivets would pop out, and they would have to run around and stick the pencils in the holes, to keep the water out.

One time he said his PBY delivered General MacArthur's revised plans for the invasion of the Philippines to Admiral Halsey's Third Fleet headquarters, and the crew couldn't help but notice that on the way to the drop-off point they had no less than six fighter escorts, but on the way home they were entirely on their own.

Fortunately, with Jackie, Betsy, Brian, and others' help, Jim wrote up his memoir of World War II in a very readable book, which I've read a couple of times. I also have recorded several hours of Jim and Von talking about their Navy and life experiences, which is on YouTube.

After hearing some of these stories and all the things he survived, I always kidded Jim that to me he was like a Powerball winner to still be here, because my dad, James Robert Callahan, was born a year later, and Jim lived 27 years longer than my dad to just short of 100, which means he had almost a quarter longer lifespan than many of his contemporaries. That's a gift for which he was thankful, and we can all be thankful.

Like most people I suppose, I'd ask Jim to what he attributed his long life, and he said that when he was at Cargill he'd get up early beforehand, and jog 2 miles before work. Even when he got older he would go out for walks when he could. Many of us saw on WCCO two years ago, a story that on one of his walks around the neighborhood he encountered a polite, 10 year old, August Riebe, who in a very loud voice thanked him for his service, and they became good friends.

Jim had some serious bouts with malaria and some other health issues, but overall, he was blessed with good health and a sharp, curious, inquiring mind during his life. He gave many excellent public talks, some of which were recorded.

We went to movies, museums, the theater, holiday parties, boat rides. We took road trips to aviation museums and other aviation events, and it was always a great pleasure to talk to Jim because of his truly encyclopedic knowledge, his thoughtfulness about history and life, and his great sense of humor. He was always interesting and fun to talk to, and he was a great friend.

Jim and Von's "generation was united not only by a common purpose" [during WWII] "but by common values—duty, honor," [frugality], "courage, service, love of family and country," [modesty, dignity, and] responsibility for oneself.* His philosophy was also in part that life is a gift, and you should appreciate the present moment.

Jim, of course, was first and foremost a family man. As he wrote in his first book, Von was the love of his life, and he

---

*— Brokaw, Tom. *The Greatest Generation*. Random House, 1998.

was very proud of his six children and their many descendants and his very large family. He always looked forward to the family reunions and gatherings in Le Mars, Iowa.

Jim spoke about the profound effect that learning about his family history, and especially his great grandfather, James Alexander McDougall, had had on him. His great grandfather's reasons for volunteering during the Civil War seemed similar to those Jim had had for serving during World War II. He valued his family's history, serving to protect the country, and he wanted that remembered, and he wrote other books about his family history.

I think if you want to see Jim and Von's legacy, all you really need to do is to look around you today or attend a family reunion or gathering.

In closing, I think Jim and Von would like to be remembered as people who lived good, blessed, happy, long, and productive lives. They lived truly remarkable lives during a truly remarkable period in history. When you have the opportunity, take time to share your stories and memories with each other, be kind to each other, and remember the many good things that they did.

> — Kevin L. Callahan; "James Robert McDougall: Words of Remembrance," May 26, 2023, Saint Therese Church of Deephaven.

Preface

Dear Reader,

This is my fourth and final book, describing my life from the time I was discharged from the Navy in 1946, up to the present day (in 2023). It covers my college years and my four years of teaching Vocational Agriculture in northwest Iowa, from 1946 through 1955. It also covers my 33-year career with Cargill's Animal Nutrition Division, from my being hired in 1955, through my retirement in 1988. In addition, the book describes my 68-year-marriage to Von, the love of my life, and the raising of our six children, whom we referred to as "Our Diamonds." The book ends with a chapter summarizing the highlights of my travels, including those associated with my business career and those involving my personal life.

My first book, *Almost Famous*, is a memoir about growing up on a farm outside of Le Mars, Iowa, from the time

of my birth in 1923, to the bombing of Pearl Harbor in 1941, marking the United States' official entrance into World War II—as well as my own. *Almost Famous* describes the profound influences that being raised on a farm and being grounded in agriculture had on my life. My second book, *Conflict to Combat in the South Pacific,* tells the story of my time spent in naval aerial combat in World War II, where I served as a combat aircrewman, ordnanceman, and bombardier in New Guinea and the Philippines. My third book, *The Road to Love, Our Family's Story 1818-1999,* describes how my ancestors came to this great country, put down roots in northwest Iowa, grew and flourished.

My fourth book, *Getting It Right: Reflections on a Life Spanning a Century,* is the last installment of my memoirs. As someone who has lived close to 100 years now, I find myself reflecting often upon a life which I feel has been long, fruitful and rewarding. I consider myself a most fortunate man to have lived so long, married the love of my life and raised 6 wonderful children, who have given me a total of 17 grandchildren and 10 great-grandchildren—and counting. I have experienced so many blessings in my life, including good health, a loving and supportive family, a first-rate education, a rewarding and distinguished career, as well as countless opportunities for travel and adventure. I have had the honor and privilege of serving in the military during WWII, and this has given me a deep appreciation of how lucky we are to live in this great country, with all its freedoms and responsibilities.

In sharing my stories, I wanted to pass on my legacy to my family, my friends, and to anyone else who might be interested. As I go through the books, I attempt to describe the events that shaped my life and formed my character. In witnessing world-wide events throughout the past 100 years, I have seen seismic changes and amazing advances, which have spanned the Great Depression, World War II, and the dawn of the 21st century. My life started out in the horse and buggy days and has lasted through the explosion of science and technology, including such tremendous accomplishments as sending men and women into the vast frontiers of space, exponentially increasing the world's food supply, and learning to treat and cure countless diseases and ailments. Of course, I am as keenly aware as anyone of the formidable challenges that lie ahead of us, as Americans and as citizens of the world.

My aim in writing my books was to share many of my experiences over the past 100 years, partly to entertain the reader and capture memories for my family, but also to pass on the many valuable lessons and insights that I have learned first-hand while witnessing so many life-changing events. In *Almost Famous,* these lessons involved growing up on a farm, developing strong family values, learning all about agriculture, and developing a solid work ethic. In *Conflict to Combat in the South Pacific,* it was about having a key role in a naval squadron defending our country overseas against a fierce enemy during WWII. In *The Road to Love*, it was about the importance of learning about the ancestors who have come before me. And finally, in *Getting It Right*, it is about raising a family in the post war years and being a critical part of revolutionizing the cattle industry by helping to bring science and technology to the business of animal feed.

My hope for you as a reader is that you will have, or will continue to have, experiences in your life that are so challenging, fulfilling and exciting, that you will want to capture them by putting them down in writing and sharing them with others, as I have. As the great philosopher Plato put it so many years ago, "Those who tell the stories, rule the world."

Chapter One:
The College Years

The Days Following Discharge from the Navy
The ranks were thinning in the Navy. The discharges were coming through, and in the fall of 1945, I was notified that I would be discharged in January of 1946. I was given orders to report to the Naval Air Technical Training Center (NATTC) in Memphis, Tennessee, where men were being mustered out.

Immediately following my discharge, I boarded the train in Memphis and headed for Chicago where I was to meet up with my fiancé, Von. The train to Chicago was what we called a regulation train trip, which was carrying lots of sailors, who were being discharged from the service. We started out down in Memphis where the weather was very

Returning from the South Pacific after WWII, Honolulu, 1944; I am on the far left.

mild, and consequently, we didn't need a heated car. In fact, the air conditioning was turned on for us. We were about halfway to Chicago when it began to get cold, and the AC was turned off. As it continued to get colder, the heat was turned on, but before too long, the temperature in the train started to get a bit too warm. The sailors were taking off their jerseys and hanging them up on hooks. The train stopped at a town just before we came to Chicago, and a small group of ladies boarded the train. They were heading into the city to shop. As they were walking through our car, they spotted those sailors with their jerseys hanging up in various stages of disarray. One of the ladies stuck her nose up in the air and announced, "Well, I'm not riding in *this* car!" I heard some sailor down at the end of the row reply, "Well, too damn bad about you, lady!"

We finally arrived in Chicago, where my fiancé, Von, and I had arranged to meet and where we would be visiting my maternal Aunt Evelyn and her friend Leona. Von would be arriving from her home in Marshalltown, Iowa. Von was a WAVE during WWII (Women Accepted for Volunteer Emergency Service, a division of the U.S. Navy created during WWII). She had been out of the service for a while, as she had received an honorable hardship discharge from the Navy when her mother had died in 1944 after a battle with tuberculosis. After leaving the Navy, Von returned home to spend some time with her family.

My Aunt Evelyn and her friend Leona lived in a very nice apartment in Chicago on the shores of Lake Michigan. The two of them took it upon themselves to give Von and me a tour of Chicago and show us around some of their favorite haunts, including a couple of nightclubs that they had visited. One of the nightclubs was called Joker Joe's. We went in and sat down at our table, very near the restrooms. I noticed a lady go over to the restroom. She took hold of the doorknob and pulled on it, but the doorknob was attached to a chain. As she kept pulling on the doorknob, more and more of the chain came out of the door, but the door wouldn't open. The lady was getting very embarrassed. Finally she figured out that the doorknob was fake, and that the door actually opened by pushing on it. We learned that one of the reasons so many customers frequented this restaurant was to watch people get embarrassed by a variety of pranks. Joker Joe himself sat up in a little control room and would peruse the crowd. If he noticed that someone had not gone to the restroom for a while, he would sound a siren and then run over to them with a small potty in his hand and place it under their chair. Then he would put his hand up to his ear like he was listening. This of course, humiliated the person being singled out.

Von got a kick out of this place. She informed me that inside the women's restroom, there was a large poster of a man on the wall, and he had a movable fig leaf covering his private parts. If a lady would lift up the fig leaf, the eyes of the man in the poster would start flashing, and a siren would sound loudly in the dining area. The guilty culprit would then have to slink out of the bathroom, fully aware that most of the patrons knew exactly what she had just done! Joker Joe's was quite an amusing place. We went to several fun places with Aunt Evelyn and Leona, and we really enjoyed our time in Chicago. After a few days, it was time for both of us to head home to our respective towns in Iowa. Von took the bus back to Marshalltown, and I took the train back to Sioux City, and then returned to Le Mars.

With Von (in center) and friends at the Skyroom at the Peabody Hotel during one of Von's visits to Memphis in 1945. Ray Roe Radney (far right) was a good friend of mine at the Naval Training Station for Aviation Maintenance in Memphis.

Developments on My Family's Farm

I returned home to our family farm in Le Mars, Iowa, in February, 1946. These were turbulent times for farmers. During the war, the government had frozen the price of livestock and had assured the farmers that they would receive at least $17.75 per hundredweight in government subsidies for their fat cattle, before the controls were removed. The controls were scheduled to be removed around the first of March, 1946, and shortly before that, my dad and I took a trip to visit the stockyards in Sioux City. There were trucks lined up as far as the eye could see. Farmers wanted to be sure to get that $17.75 per hundredweight government subsidy. Some arrived just under the wire.

As luck would have it, beginning that next week, cattle prices starting going up, and within about two or three weeks, the price of cattle had doubled from the $17.75 per hundredweight subsidy that had previously been promised by the government. So all of those farmers who had rushed to get in on the subsidy ended up losing a lot of money by not waiting and selling at a higher price.

With livestock prices temporarily frozen by the government, my dad was under the impression that, like the cattle, hogs would rise in price after the government removed the controls, so he decided to take advantage of this by breeding additional gilts (young female hogs). He was

Chapter One: The College Years

Getting reacquainted with some of my siblings after returning from the war; (from left to right) Janice, Nick, me, Eydie, and Denny.

planning to sell a certain number of them as bred sows. Under normal circumstances, my dad would have bred about 16 sows and farrowed them out, but this spring he bred about 40 sows with the intention of selling the additional 24 gilts and making a profit.

So now we were in the market to sell bred gilts. Dad took them down to the sale barn, but they didn't bring the price that he thought they ought to, so he brought them back home. He then ran an ad in the paper that read "Bred Sows for Sale". The market price at that time was around $90 to $95 per head, but my dad hadn't stated a price in the ad; he just indicated that the sows were for sale.

My brother, Doug, and I were in the yard at the farm getting ready to do some mowing when a car with Sioux County plates drove up with four farmers in it. One of them got out, and my dad walked over to him.

The farmer said, "I understand you have bred sows for sale."

My dad replied, "Yes I do."

The farmer inquired, "What are you asking for them?"

Now bear in mind that you could buy bred sows at this time for about $90 to $95 apiece, but my dad threw out his price as $125. He believed in the bartering system, and he would start high and then work the price down to what the customer was actually willing to give him. He figured you can always go down in price, but you can't go back up.

Chapter One: The College Years

Well, that farmer never gave my dad a chance. He just turned on his heel, got back in the car, slammed the door, drove away, and that was that. We didn't have any other takers on the ad.

A few days later, my dad called up his brother, my uncle Jack Sr., who had a truck. My dad asked Jack to come out to the farm and help him take the bred sows to the sale barn. Jack came out, but he had stopped first in Struble, and I think he had had a few drinks too many.

It was March of 1946. The ground had thawed, and the yard was very soft. On our farm, in order to load the animals, you had to back up to the barn door. When Jack backed up the truck, it was fairly light, because it didn't have a load yet. However, when the truck was loaded up, it was much heavier. Once Jack started to drive the truck out of the yard, it sank down into the soft mud and manure and got stuck.

My dad was getting impatient about this time, because he didn't think Jack was driving the truck right, and that's why he had gotten stuck. So Dad went and got the tractor to pull the truck out. Then the tractor got stuck too.

We did get the tractor out, but by that time, my dad had had enough and he yelled, "Just pull the end gate up and dump the hogs out!" And that's what we did. We pulled the end gate up and chased the hogs out of the truck through that mess of mud and manure, and Jack went home.

That left us with more than twice as many sows as we would normally farrow out. Our hog barn held about a dozen sows, and we could put a few more of them in the alleyway, but those were the only facilities we had to farrow sows. Now all of a sudden, we had an extra 24 sows that we needed to put somewhere to farrow. In those days, each sow had to have her own pen to farrow her piglets. So we had to make extra pens all over the place: in the horse barn, in the cattle barn—wherever we could possibly make pens!

The next problem we encountered was that we didn't have water or feed near some of these pens, so we had to haul all of the water and feed in five-gallon buckets. Each of us would carry two five-gallon buckets at a time—that's about 80 pounds of water per trip! We'd water the sows, and then haul feed into each of their pens.

That summer of 1946 was really a struggle for us on the farm, especially finding pens for all those sows, keeping them fed and watered, and farrowing them out. Through all this we wound up with a lot more sows than my dad ever anticipated having. This was the same farm that my brother Doug's family owns and farms now. My dad had purchased the 250 acre farm the previous fall, in 1945, for $130 an acre. At about $32,500, this was a very large expenditure for my dad, so he had borrowed a down payment from his sister-in-law, my Aunt Evelyn.

Chapter One: The College Years

Aerial view of my folks' farm in Le Mars, Iowa, which my brother Doug and his sons Shayne and Miles took over farming in the 1970s. Top photo is from 2016; bottom from 1973.

Checking on the cattle at our family farm in the 1950s.

Throughout that summer, the price of hogs kept going up. So Dad decided to hold onto those pigs, and we fed them out to between 300 and 400 hundred pounds each. By market time in the late fall of 1946, we had about 300 pigs at an average of 350 pounds each. Dad got $27.00 a hundredweight. If you multiply that out, you'll see that he almost paid for the entire farm with that one batch of pigs.

It is ironic that my dad worried so much about getting the farm paid for. In buying the farm, my dad took on what he considered to be a substantial amount of debt. As luck would have it, through this chance series of events involving the delayed sale of the pigs in the summer of 1946, my dad ended up essentially paying for most of the farm in one year!

The Wedding and Newlywed Phase

Around this time, another very important event was shaping up in my life. June 9th, 1946, was the date Von and I had set for our wedding. We decided on a small and simple ceremony. We were married midday by Father LaVelle

Von (second from the left) at one of the picnics at my folks' farm. My Aunt Mary is on Von's right and my mom, Edith, is on Von's left.

in the rectory at St. James Catholic Church in Le Mars. Von wore a blue suit. My sister Mabel, was Von's Maid of Honor. We had asked my cousin, Clyde Keough, to be my best man, but Clyde wasn't able to be there, so Mabel's friend, Gordon Burkett, took Clyde's place. I didn't know Gordon that well, but I remembered him from my high school days.

We were all ready to go, but an unfortunate event happened. Von's dad, Roy, and her three siblings, Gerrie, Patsy and Bill, were supposed to arrive in Le Mars from Marshalltown that morning, but their train was delayed in Council Bluffs, so they couldn't make it on time for the wedding ceremony. Von felt bad for her dad, as it seemed that he was often unlucky. Her family members did arrive in time for the celebration afterward, however. My parents hosted a wonderful picnic wedding reception under the big trees out at our farm.

That same evening, Von and I boarded the train out of Le Mars and headed east for Clear Lake, Iowa, near Mason City. We arrived in Clear Lake where my second cousin, Bobby Moran, met us and brought us to the lake. He had arranged for us to stay a few days in a little summer cottage that he rented out each summer.

The cottage was located right on Clear Lake. That afternoon we went swimming, and then Von and I attended a dance at the Surf Ballroom, which is the place where

Chapter One: The College Years

With Von (right), on our honeymoon, seated with Mr. and Mrs. Oscar Fewins, at the Surf Ballroom in Clear Lake, Iowa, June, 1946. I met Oscar when we were both in the Iowa State Guard, where he was a sergeant.

Buddy Holly would later give his last performance before being killed in the tragic plane crash near Clear Lake, on February 3rd, 1959.

While we were in Clear Lake, Bobby introduced us to Earl McDermot, who lived in Mason City and worked for Cargill. Earl had married my great aunt Annie Moran's daughter, Marie. This is the first I had heard the name of Cargill Incorporated, and I soon learned about what a large company it was.

Von and I enjoyed the better part of a week together on our honeymoon at Clear Lake, but then it was time to return to Le Mars. There was a lot of work to do on the farm.

The Chester and Edith McDougall Family circa late 1940s. Back row (from left to right): Doug, Mabel, Bill, me, Dick. Front Row: Nick, Janice, Mark on Chester's (Chet's) lap, Edith, Eydie, Denny.

While in Le Mars, we stayed occasionally at my Aunt Mary's house in town, but we spent most of our time at the farm. My paternal grandmother, Martha Warren McDougall, had grown up in England. She had more than a passing acquaintance with the battlefields in England, and she was keenly aware of the human costs of war. She had passed away soon after I left for the service. I felt badly, because she had been very worried about me. I wish she could have known that I would make it back safely.

Chapter One: The College Years

Von now had time to get acquainted with my family. By 1946 my parents had 10 children; myself (age 23), Mabel (21), Bill (19), Dick (15), Doug (12), Janice (8), Eydie (5), Nick (4), Denny (2), and Mark (1). Most of my siblings who were old enough to do chores were still in school, and Dad needed help from the older kids. Aunt Mary, my dad's sister, would come out to the farm frequently to work in our garden, gather eggs, and help with the kids. Mary and Von were a huge help to my mom.

Von enjoyed staying on the farm, and she got along very well with my family. She and my mother enjoyed listening to soap operas, such as "Helen Trent" and "My Gal Sunday," while they cooked big meals for the men out working on the farm. Von really looked up to my mother as a role model, especially since Von had just lost her own mother about two years before in 1944. Von was also the first in-law introduced into our immediate family, so there was a learning curve involved on the part of both Von and my family. My brother Nick, who was about four years old when Von joined our family, was not too crazy about Von at first when she sat in the chair at the dining room table, next to my mother, that he had become accustomed to sitting in. Von's home-made spaghetti recipe that she got from her Italian friends at Yankton College definitely helped win Nick over—as well as earning her some brownie points with the rest of the family. Of course, her endearing ways and winning personality also factored in!

Sunday dinner on my parents' farm in the 1950s.

At harvest time, my younger brother, Doug, and I would go out and pick up a load of bundles of grain and drive it in. Doug would drive the horses, while I would throw the bundles onto the hay rack to take in to the threshing machine. This same threshing machine was used by a ring of about seven neighboring farms all around the same time. I remember it was the hottest time of the year, and Doug and I were working hard. We'd fill up with water, and we'd feel like a couple of cream cans full of liquid sloshing around inside of us. On top of that, we'd be full of food from the enormous meals that all the farmers' wives would prepare for us, where they would all be trying to outdo each other. Then we'd drive back out into the field to resume working.

Chapter One: The College Years

Life at Yankton College

After the war, Von and I decided to take advantage of the G.I. Bill for Veterans, and I enrolled in Yankton College in Yankton, South Dakota. Von was also planning to attend college but decided to wait awhile, since she was expecting our first baby.

With the war having just ended, Von and I were among the multitude of veterans being discharged all at once, so many G.I.'s were in the same boat—enrolling in colleges and universities all at the same time. I started attending Yankton College in 1946, and graduated in 1949 with a B.A. degree (majoring in Biology and minoring in Education). Then, later on in 1949, Von and I moved to Brookings, South Dakota, where I earned a B.S. Degree in Agricultural Education at South Dakota State University (SDSU) in 1951. Von took journalism classes at both Yankton and South Dakota State.*

ENROLLING

One day, in spring of 1946, I ran into an old friend from high school, Mark Meis, and I told him I was thinking about going to school to earn a degree in veterinary medicine. Mark suggested that we check out Iowa State University, the main school in Iowa for that kind of training. The

---

*— SDSU College of Agriculture, Food and Environmental Sciences was called South Dakota State College during the period of time when Von and I attended classes.

two of us drove to Ames, and Mark introduced me to the Admissions Director at Iowa State, who asked me what he could do for me. I said, "Well, I'm interested in going to school here." And he looked at me rather condescendingly and replied, "Yeah—you and a lot of other guys." After hesitating a moment I said, "You know, I think I just changed my mind." Then Mark and I left abruptly and went home. I didn't really want to go to school where they took you for granted, which apparently they could afford to do at Iowa State, because it was an extremely popular school. I'm sure there were plenty of applicants lined up to take my place.

Shortly after that incident, I ran into my old boss, Mike Means. He was in town and was in the process of closing his Valet Cleaners business in Le Mars (where I had worked during high school). Mike had moved to Yankton, South Dakota, to take over his father's cleaning business, as his father was recently deceased. Mike asked me to consider working part-time for him while I attended college, and I accepted his offer.

During the summer of 1946, I traveled to Yankton to look over Mike's new operation, and I also went over to Yankton College and talked to Dr. Shock at the Admissions Office.

Dr. Shock welcomed me with open arms and told me he would like me to go to school there. He also gave me information about their Veterans Housing Program, which at that time consisted of seven trailers and a central building that housed the lavatories and fuel storage. The trailers that made up Yankton's veterans housing had come from the WWII Marine Base at Cherry Point, Rhode Island, and they were not in very good shape.

WINTER OF 1946-47

As it happened, the winter of 1946-47 was a bitterly cold one, and unfortunately, the trailers we vets were living in at Yankton College were not designed for cold weather. The wind would blow underneath the units and make the floors very cold. I had to haul in lots of fuel oil and pour it into the little heating stove in our trailer. Von and I had a little two-burner electric stove to cook on, and we also had a small metal oven that we could put on top of the two burners. We'd turn the burners on and heat the oven; that was how we did our cooking. We had no indoor running water, no toilets or other amenities in that trailer. I remember one particular night, it was brutally cold, and we ran out of fuel oil. I had to go out and get more fuel. Then I poured it into the stove, and suddenly the stove caught on fire! I immediately grabbed ahold of the stove and threw it outside. After that it got even colder inside the trailer. We figured if anything could have frozen up, it would have, but we didn't really have anything in the trailer to freeze up except us!

Fortunately for Von and me, in the spring of 1947, Yankton College built six new duplexes, which amounted to a dozen veteran housing units all together. Von and I qualified for one of these units, and they were really nice. They had two bedrooms, a bathroom with a toilet and a shower, city water, city sewage system, and central gas heat. We didn't have a refrigerator, but we did have an ice box, and we had to drill a little hole in the floor so that the melted ice water could drain out. Needless to say, our ice box wasn't the coldest thing in the world, but we figured that wasn't bad for our second year at Yankton College. All in all, we counted our blessings.

MY DISASTROUS CHEMISTRY EXPERIMENT
Because so many veterans were getting discharged from the military at that time and enrolling in college all at once, the facilities were becoming overloaded, and as a result, if you didn't get to your school and sign up for your courses ahead of time and get your books arranged for, you could easily wind up without a textbook for your class. If you didn't have a textbook, you had to try to find a fellow classmate who did. Then you'd try to study with them, so you'd find out what was in the book.

This is precisely the predicament I found myself in with my chemistry class in Yankton. I developed a sort of "monkey-see, monkey-do" approach in the chemistry lab, where I would watch my fellow students—the ones whom I thought knew something about what they were doing. And I would do what they did. One of the first experiments that we tried in the laboratory was constructing hydrogen generators, which we made by taking hydrochloric acid and mixing it with aluminum. Then we would combine this mixture in a test tube. As the chloride was exposed to the aluminum, it gave off explosive hydrogen gas.

There was a Bunsen burner set up off to the side. As I watched, my classmates were taking test tubes and testing this gas as it was being emitted. They would get a test tube full of gas and then take it over to the Bunsen burner, and if it popped, that indicated that there was still too much oxygen in the generator to produce pure hydrogen gas.

I was watching this one particular student, who was holding his test tube over the burner for brief intervals. Since he still had some oxygen in his test tube, it made a popping noise. This guy was going back and forth, checking to make sure that the gas didn't pop anymore in the test tube before he held it over the burner for a more prolonged period. I took my test tube over, and it popped. Because I had no book and didn't know any better, I assumed the popping meant the test tube was ready. At that point, I picked up the burner and held it up to my test tube. Unfortunately, my test tube (would-be hydrogen generator) blew up! There was a very loud explosion that cleaned off our entire lab table, and it drove my test tube right into the wall. It was as if a fire alarm went off, and the instructor, Dr. Evans, came running over and shouted, "Out, out, out!" He didn't give me a chance to explain; he just kicked me right out of class!

Shortly afterwards, one of my classmates came up and told me, "Dr. Evans would like to see you." So I went in to see Dr. Evans. After he calmed down and thought about it, he said that he realized what had happened—the explosion occurred because I didn't have a textbook. After I finally did acquire a textbook, Dr. Evans and I became good friends, and ironically, it turned out that some of my best grades at Yankton were in chemistry.

LESSONS IN FINANCES

Before too long, Von and I decided that we needed to develop a household budget. We both received monthly stipend checks as part of the GI Bill that allowed us modest living expenses while attending college. We came to the realization that if we were going to make it through college, we had to have a budget to make our cash last through the end of each month. Von and I didn't know the first thing about budgets, but we had to start somewhere. One of our initial ideas about a budget was to keep a record of everything we spent, so we started to write everything down. If we spent a nickel for an ice cream

Oct 1946	1	Cash on hand	61
	1	groceries	1.35
	1	milk	.31
	2	ice cream	.60
	2	groceries	1.24
	3	cigarettes	.20
	3	milk	.31
	3	groceries	1.74
	4	taxi	.40
	5	milk	.30
	5	hairpins, toothpaste, soap	.75
	5	groceries	3.83
	5	bakery	1.00
	5	ice	.12
	5	groceries	1.31
	7	groceries	2.06
	7	milk	.15
	7	groceries	1.48
	8	groceries	1.14
	9	milk	.31
	10	cigarettes	.20
	10	postcards	.03
	10	groceries	1.52
	10	Glo Coat	.59
	10	prescription	2.00
	10	jewel tea	1.83
	11	milk	.31
	11	groceries	1.80
	12	cooker	12.22
	12	food	1.28
	12	groceries + meat	5.00
	14	—	—
	15	milk	.31

Sample of our family budget in 1946.

~~16 government check~~	~~47 00~~	
~~18 groceries~~		3 00
~~18 paper~~		
16 government check	47 00	
18 groceries	3 00	
18 paper	30	
19 College Homecoming dance	3 50	
19 groceries	4 50	
20 Dinner & movie	2 00	
21		
22 groceries	5 00	
24 groceries	1 50	
24 wet mop	1 50	
25 groceries	1 17	
26 milk	16	
26 paper	30	
26 misc'l	2 50	
28 groceries	2 78	
28 Valet Cleaners	5 00	
29 groceries	90	
30 groceries	3 00	
31 groceries	2 00	
31 Insurance (J.S.)	13 00	
31 Insurance (Travelers)	17 27	
Nov. 1 groceries	2 50	
1 paper	30	
1 misc'l	3 00	
2 groceries	2 23	
4 groceries	2 80	

Sample of our family budget in 1946, continued.

cone, or a dime for a carton of milk, we wrote it down. That was how we budgeted.

Of course, toward the end of the month, as often happens to couples just starting out in life, Von and I would tend to run short of money, so we would start rummaging through the furniture and digging down between the sofa and chair cushions trying to find loose pocket change to buy food. We would try to scrounge up enough money to cook a big pot of chili, and then we would make that chili last for a week. We often had chili for breakfast and chili for lunch and chili for supper!

Von and I also had some aluminum pans, and we would keep that chili in the those pans and store them in the ice box. After a while, we discovered that the chili was corroding the bottom of these pans. Common sense told us that this practice couldn't be too good for our health. So we were in a quandary about how to store this chili in order to make it last a long time.

Something that helped stretch our money was the fact that we had some friends who hunted pheasants during hunting season on weekends, and if they got lucky, they'd bring us pheasants that they had shot. Sometimes, they'd be drinking and we'd be in bed. They'd just hang the game on our doorknob, and they knew we'd dress the game and cook it for them. They'd come over—usually the next day, and Von would cook up a feast.

While Von and I were attending classes at Yankton, Mike Means gradually increased my hours at the Valet Cleaners to the point where I was working 20 hours a week, as well as going to school full-time. Working so much didn't pan out very well in the long run, because I suspected I was starting to develop an ulcer. I was burning the candle at both ends, and it was interfering with my school work. So I made what I believed was a wise decision and cut way back on my hours at the Valet Cleaners.

OUR NEW REFRIGERATOR

During midwinter of 1947, while in the midst of taking classes, I realized I needed a little extra help with my math studies, and I had struck up an acquaintance with a fellow named Mac McKeever, who was really sharp at math. He would come over to the duplex and tutor me at our kitchen table, and in return for the favor, Von would sometimes invite him to eat lunch with us. Around this time, during a visit to the doctor, I was warned that I could soon get an ulcer if I didn't stop eating greasy food. Von and I had already bought some bacon, and we had put it in our icebox.

About three weeks later, I invited Mac to come over to study, and I tempted him by telling him that we would fix him a nice breakfast afterwards. I was thinking that we would serve him the bacon we had in our icebox. After we were finished studying, Von fried up some bacon and eggs. Mac, who seemed to be very hungry, readily accepted our offer of breakfast. After he'd eaten, he thanked us and told us that the food was delicious. Then he left. I didn't see Mac again for a couple of days. He ended up getting very sick, which Von and I strongly suspected was from eating the bacon that had been starting to spoil in our "not so cold" icebox. Not surprisingly, Mac didn't come back over for a while.

After that unfortunate experience, Von and I figured out that we were probably going to have to make proper storage of cold food a priority, and we purchased our first refrigerator. It cost $204. We had a heck of a time paying for that purchase—plus we still didn't have a car. It turned out that a friend of mine, Bob Peterson, had a car for sale. It was a 1937 Ford V8 two-door, and Bob sold the car to me for $1100, which I thought was a good deal. So then Von and I could drive back home to Le Mars, which was a very welcome development—and also, we had a baby on the way, another very welcome development!

OUR FIRST DAUGHTER, DANA, IS BORN

In early March of 1947, Von was nine months pregnant, and she had a good friend by the name of Kay Kurvink, who lived in the adjoining part of our duplex. Kay's husband, Bud, was the quarterback on the college football team, and Von and I socialized with the Kurvinks as a couple quite a bit.

This was the first time Von had ever been pregnant and she didn't know exactly what to expect. One day, I got home and found that Kay had taken Von to the hospital.

Earlier in the day, when Von was just waking up, she told me she felt like she was going to have the baby soon, and I replied, "No you're not. That baby isn't due for five more days." Later, after I left for class, Von discovered she had started bleeding. She knocked on the Kurvink's wall, because we had adjoining units in the duplex, and she yelled, "Kay, I think I'm having a miscarriage." Kay rushed over and said, "No, you aren't having a miscarriage. You're having a baby!" Bud and I had just gone to school, so Kay drove Von to the hospital, and sure enough, our first child, Dana, was born shortly afterward.

Then in the summer of 1947, Von, who was majoring in journalism, started taking summer school classes. I was taking summer school classes also, and now that we had baby Dana, we needed to find a babysitter. Von and I found out about an older couple, who had a big house over on the edge of campus, and they agreed to babysit Dana. Von and I went over to their house to look it over, and we discovered that this couple raised and sold parakeets. I asked to see the parakeets, so I was escorted upstairs, and the birds were just flying free and loose up there. Parakeets

Chapter One: The College Years

Bonding with little Dana in Yankton in 1947.

With Von and Dana in front of our veterans' housing unit at Yankton College.

were all over the place! When the couple wanted to sell some of the parakeets, they would just go upstairs and catch however many birds they needed.

Dana stayed with this couple who had the parakeets while Von and I went to classes. The child care arrangements weren't full-time. We just needed a babysitter when Von's classes conflicted with mine. Von and I would try to schedule our classes so that we could take turns caring for Dana.

Von and I really enjoyed Yankton. We made a lot of nice friends there. We also had family members visit from Le Mars. I recall that my Aunt Mary came over to see Dana, and my brother Bill stopped by occasionally to visit.

Life at South Dakota State University

After I graduated with a B.A. in Biology and Education at Yankton, I decided I needed additional schooling to make myself more desirable in the job market, so I enrolled at South Dakota State College, which is now called South Dakota State University (SDSU) in Brookings, to earn a B.S. in Agricultural Education. I figured this way, I could expand my employment options, and I could get a job in either teaching or business. Von and I both ended up attending SDSU.

One of the advantages Von and I had was that both of us were WWII veterans, and wherever we went, the college administration could report that there were two veterans in one unit for their government housing program. South Dakota State University was quite agreeable to having Von and me enroll, and we were told that they would also make veterans' housing available for us. So Von and I got in our car, which was that same old beat-up Ford 1937 V-8 that had several hundred thousand miles on it, and we drove up to Brookings to check out SDSU's veterans' housing arrangements with little Dana, who was now three years old.

When we arrived at SDSU, we went to the house of the manager, Mr. Perry, who was in charge of Veterans' Housing. It was about 7:00 in the evening that very cold winter night when Von and I knocked on his door. He told us that Dana could stay at his house with his family while he showed Von and me the available housing units. So we left Dana behind at the Perrys' nice warm house while we went over to check out the vacant single trailer, intended to be only a temporary overnight place for us to stay until we had secured our permanent arrangements. There was no electricity in this trailer, and we had to use a flashlight. Mr. Perry showed the unit to us, and we took him up on his offer to let us stay overnight in the trailer.

Von and I carried our suitcases in and took out our nightclothes. Then we had to go to get Dana from the Perry's house. When we picked up Dana, she was all giggly and excited, because she thought she was finally going to her new "real" home like the one she left in Yankton. So we arrived at this trailer that was dark and cold and off by itself—no lights, no heat, no water, no bathroom, no nothing. Dana took one look at the place and asked in a very disappointed and incredulous little voice, "Is this where we're gonna live?!" Although she was little, she knew this definitely wasn't where she wanted to stay.

After Von and I started school at SDSU, we'd have some of the guys who were our friends come over, and they'd babysit Dana. Dana went to school at SDSU too. She was in a teacher training class as a little student, and she really enjoyed it. She loved all the people and was happy as a lark.

While finishing up our college years at SDSU, Von and I developed many good friends, and I had some excellent professors in the Agricultural Education (Ag Ed) Department. Two that I distinctly recall were Dr. Stan Sundet and Dr. Jim Kaiser. Stan Sundet was the Ag Ed Director at SDSU. He taught the Ag Ed class that I was in, and he supervised me in my student teaching. Dr. Sundet provided me with a lot of guidance as I prepared to launch my own teaching career as a vocational agriculture instructor.

Another exceptionally strong program at SDSU was livestock judging, which was headed up by Professor Jim Kaiser. Jim Kaiser knew livestock and was able to communicate to the class exactly what it was he was looking for in various animals and why. His instruction left a vivid impression on me, which I put to good use later on when Stan Sundet assigned me to do my student teaching through SDSU under Mr. Allen Doberstein in Alcester, South Dakota, a town of about 900 people.

Mr. Doberstein had a very active and strong chapter of the Future Farmers of America (FFA). Although I already had a pretty good idea of what the organization was about, this was really the first time that I was able to see FFA in action. I quickly learned more about FFA's activities, including all of the great competitions and contests, as well as fund-raising initiatives, which served as valuable learning opportunities for the members.

Chapter Two:
The Teaching Years

Interviewing for Teaching Positions
I graduated from South Dakota State University (SDSU), in 1951 with a B.S. degree in Agricultural Education and immediately started looking for teaching positions. I found out upon my graduation from SDSU that reputable high schools needing full-time vocational agriculture instructors were few and far between. Bear in mind that teaching Vocational Agriculture (Vo Ag) was a 12-month job, because in addition to working through the school year, it entailed working with boys during the summertime when they were involved in various seasonal projects. The job also required conducting agriculture classes with established farmers. These adult classes were usually taught in the evenings.

A picture taken during my teaching years. I taught for a total of four years (from 1951 through 1955) in consolidated school districts for small towns in northwestern Iowa. I taught in a split school arrangement between two schools, Hayes and Sulphur Springs, for two years. For the third year, I taught in Sulphur Springs alone. For the fourth year, I taught in Kingsley.

Two of the schools I recall that had openings when I was looking for my first teaching position in 1951 were located in the northwest corner of South Dakota, Buffalo and Lemon High Schools. Both Buffalo and Lemon were in towns with populations of about 1400. Buffalo was offering a salary of $3600 for a 12-month Vo Ag instructor, and Lemon was offering slightly more—$3700 for a 12-month position of the same nature. At that time, I had a wife and a child, and I didn't relish the prospect of living on $300 a month. That was about what I had received as a student at Yankton College and SDSU in the form of my monthly GI benefit payment and job salary, so I continued to look around.

My First Teaching Position in Hayes and Sulfur Springs, Iowa

After checking out the jobs in Buffalo and Lemon, I went on to interview at several other schools in northwest Iowa. Because I had grown up in northwest Iowa, this area attracted my interest. I ended up finding a position serving two consolidated school districts in northwest Iowa—both small rural districts. At that time a consolidated school district consisted of Grades 1 through 12. One school was called Hayes Consolidated, on the south shore of Storm Lake. The other school, Sulphur Springs

Consolidated, was located six miles away, in the town of Sulphur Springs, which was about three and a half miles east of Storm Lake. I negotiated an arrangement with the administrators of these two schools in which I would split my time as a Vo Ag instructor between the two. I would teach a half a day at Hayes High School in the morning. Then I would drive six miles and teach in the afternoon at Sulphur Springs High School, and I would teach Hayes and Sulphur Spring's adult agriculture class in the evenings.

I basically used the same lesson plans for both school districts—duplicate plans for both of my high school

My 1953 Sulphur Springs High School Vo Ag Class working on their projects in the bus garage.

Vo Ag classes and then duplicate plans for both my adult agriculture classes. For the adult classes in the evenings, I was required to organize a board of directors consisting of selected farmers from each district, and we would sit down together and determine the topics to study. Some of the most influential farmers in the community would come to the adult evening classes and would engage in discussions and learn about different facets of agriculture.

LEARNING ABOUT INCOME TAXES THE HARD WAY
Each of the two schools, Hayes and Sulphur Springs, offered me a salary of $2300 annually, so between the two schools, my total income was $4600. The state agreed to subsidize my salary at 50% in both districts, since I was teaching four quarters between the two schools. This was the highest salary that any Vo Ag instructor who had graduated from SDSU had been offered for the first year of teaching. That was all well and good, but since this was my first full-time, salaried position outside of military service, I had some important life-lessons to learn. One valuable lesson was about income tax.

Since the two schools I worked for, Hayes and Sulphur Springs, were splitting my salary in half, neither school was deducting income tax from my salary when they paid me. This would prove to be a real problem during my first year of teaching when tax time rolled around. Up to that point in my life, I had never had to think about income tax. I didn't have to pay income tax when I was in the service, and I didn't have to pay income tax while I was going to college. So I wasn't really aware that I needed to pay income tax at all until the IRS notified me that my first tax bill was overdue.

Quite unexpectedly, I found out that I owed the government $500! Von and I didn't have anywhere near that amount of money set aside in any kind of reserve fund. Up to that time, Von and I were "rocking along," making car payments, buying groceries, and paying rent and other bills. All of a sudden, the rug got pulled right out from under us. This predicament required some serious financial problem-solving on our part.

A man named Axel Bodholtz had introduced me to the commercial banks in Storm Lake. Axel was the president of the school board in Sulphur Springs. He seemed to be the fatherly type, and he took me under his wing and introduced me around in the community when I first started teaching. Axel was a very outgoing person and very free with his advice. One of his suggestions was that I do my banking business with a bank called the Blue Bank in Storm Lake. So I went in and opened a checking account with the Blue Bank and deposited my paychecks there each month. The other bank in town was operated by a man by the name of Harry Schaller. Harry Schaller was a progressive, well-regarded banker who owned several farms in the area, and he appeared to be more prosperous and more of an aggressive salesman than the operators of the Blue Bank. In any event, not knowing very much about either bank when I first started teaching, I followed Axel's recommendation and opened my accounts with the Blue Bank.

Finding myself in quite a quandary about my tax problem, I headed to my bank, the Blue Bank, and I told the banker, "I'd like to borrow some money." Then he asked me, "Do you have any life insurance?" Well, I had life insurance at one time, but I had let it expire. (The insurance agents would take my money and put it towards Von's life insurance, and would put her money towards mine, and it seemed like it was always mixed up, so Von and I just decided to forget about it. That was how GI insurance seemed to work in those days—not very well.) So that option was out. Then the banker asked me, "How about your car?" Unfortunately, there was already a loan on my car. It was mortgaged through the First National Bank in Le Mars, so the representative at the Blue Bank said, "Well sorry—then I guess we can't do anything for you."

Of course, that did not help the situation at all, so I told the Blue Bank representative, "Then you can go ahead and close my account here, because there really isn't any point in pumping on a dry well." So the Blue Bank closed my account, which amounted to about $55, as I recall. I took the money that was left in my account, and I walked across the street to Harry Schaller's bank. I thought I might as well open an account over there. I wasn't going to continue to do business with the people at the Blue Bank, because I didn't feel that they were any help to me at all. I had already met Harry, and I knew that he was a nice guy.

So I walked over to Harry Schaller's bank, and I went up to the teller. Harry was in his office with the door open. He looked over and saw me at the teller's, and he yelled, "Hey Mac! What's goin' on?" I told him, "I'd like to open up an account here," and he said, "Oh great—come on in! How come you're switching banks?" I replied, "Well I need some money." Harry never even asked me why I needed the cash. He just reached in his desk drawer, pulled out a notepad and asked, "How much do you need?" I didn't realize it at the time, but there was some animosity between the two banks, and what was fanning the animosity was the fact that the FFA members had opened their accounts with Harry Schaller. So the Blue Bank must have been thinking, "Who the heck is this guy who's the advisor to the local Future Farmers of America Chapter and not encouraging his FFA members to bank with us?" They must have been upset with me over at the Blue Bank before I even walked in the door. Anyway, Harry had decided to invest in me and help me out with the loan for my income tax.

That was the start of a good relationship between the two of us. This experience taught me a valuable lesson about how things work in terms of doing business in a small town and about the need to save money for a rainy day.

EXPERIENCES WITH FUTURE FARMERS OF AMERICA (FFA)
When I first began teaching, I had to set up the Vo Ag Department at Hayes, but the Vo Ag Department at Sulphur Springs was already established, and they had been very happy with my predecessor, Pete Duin. The reason that I was hired at Sulphur Springs in the first place was that Pete had taken another job as a Vo Ag instructor in the nearby town of Newell. Staff members in the Sulphur Springs district would often remind me of what a great teacher Pete was, but all of a sudden, after the job change, Pete went from being a very popular figure in Sulphur Springs to being a key competitor.

Before long, my FFA Chapters in Hayes and Sulphur Springs started gaining on Newell in the area-wide competitions between the FFA's in the various school districts. For instance, at corn picking time, our FFA Chapters were invited to put on a demonstration at an agricultural festival in Newell. My chapters chose to do a safety demonstration, and the Newell chapter chose to do a demonstration that featured different kinds of grains. Newell's grain demonstration turned out to be a pretty dry topic. My students went out and got the part of a corn picker where the corn moved up by way of the conveyor belt into the picker. The students found a pair of overalls and made a dummy, and they used some large tin cans to represent the machine rollers. They put the dummy's arm in between these tin can rollers of the machine to simulate a farm accident and got some red paint and spread it all over to look like blood—farm accidents were all too common in those days. Then the students started up the rollers with an electric motor. That demonstration was pretty attention-getting and dramatic, so my students really stole the show from Pete's students in Newell.

The Hayes and Sulphur Springs boys in the FFA Chapters liked to plan a trip for a week each summer, and they had some pretty distant and elaborate places identified where they wanted to travel. They also realized that these trips cost money, so they got involved with fundraising—selling magazine subscriptions, collecting scrap metal from area farms, and raising pigs. During their FFA meetings, the boys planned where they wanted to go on field trips using the money they earned. Two trips that I recall particularly well were the trips to the Black Hills in South Dakota, and the Boundary Waters Canoe Area in northern Minnesota.

The Black Hills was a great learning opportunity, because one of my student's fathers at Hayes had a connection with a rancher in South Dakota, who sold cattle. When the

Some of my FFA students on their fieldtrip to the Badlands in the Dakotas.

rancher found out that we were traveling to the Black Hills, he invited my class to visit him on his ranch. This turned out to be a valuable educational experience for my students, and to top it all off, they were treated to some great South Dakota hospitality, as the rancher's wife cooked a delicious dinner for all of us.

Another trip that I took with my FFA students that was especially memorable was to the Boundary Waters Canoe Area. The Boundary Waters is a vast region of lakes and rivers along Minnesota's border with Canada, where only canoes are allowed—no motorboats. The boys spent a considerable amount of time planning the trip, and they started receiving a lot of information in the mail from canoe outfitters in the area. The boys decided on which outfitter they wanted to work with, and off we went to the Boundary Waters. Pete Duin took a trip to the Ozarks with his FFA students from Newell at the same time I took my students on the trip up north, so our two local groups of FFA students were both gone at the same time. Tragically, Pete had only been down in the Ozarks with his group for about three hours, when one of his boys ended up dead. Apparently, this particular boy went out in the water, didn't know how to swim and drowned.

Although fortunately we didn't lose anybody in the Boundary Waters, I certainly had my hands full with my charges. I had some real characters along on the trip. Most of the kids were Iowa farm boys who had never been very far from home before, much less anywhere without their parents. There were 23 of us on the trip—20 kids and 3 supervisors: myself, Roger Jorgenson, who was a coach at Sulphur Springs, and the bus driver. Three of the kids were from Hayes and the other 17 were from Sulphur Springs. We insisted that the boys wear life jackets whenever they were near the water, and we enforced it. We took the necessary precautions, because a lot of these boys didn't know how to swim, and we sure didn't want to lose anybody. We also tied the canoes together with ropes like catamarans so that they would be more stable, because as the old saying goes, "Boys will be boys," and we figured our charges would try to tip the canoes over if they had the opportunity.

Chapter Two: The Teaching Years

Our canoe trip started out smoothly enough. We got up to Ely, the town that is considered to be the gateway to the Boundary Waters, and we stopped at the canoe outfitters. Our outfitters made quite a production of getting everybody equipped with what they needed: canoes, paddles, life jackets, rain gear, food, water, etc. By the time we got to our starting point and launched our canoes, it was about three or four o'clock in the afternoon. It wasn't long before we came to our first portage.

None of us had ever encountered a portage before. We knew what the word meant, but not much beyond that. In order to "portage," we were required to unload the gear from the canoes and then carry the canoes and all our gear over land from one lake to another. In the Boundary Waters, the portages can vary from just a few feet to more than a mile. We didn't really know what we were doing, so as you can imagine, navigating the portages with all those boys and canoes and supplies turned out to be quite a challenge. We quickly learned that portaging requires organization, teamwork, and a lot of energy! By the time we had carried all of our canoes and supplies across that first portage, it had gotten pretty late, and everyone was very tired. Because it was growing dark, we decided to skip supper, pitch our tents, and go to bed. We planned to get up early in the morning and cook a big breakfast of bacon and eggs before starting out on a full day of canoeing. The outfitters had labeled the package of bacon, "Bear Bait," and that really got the boys' attention. Their eyes were as wide as saucers, and they blurted out "Bear bait—you mean there are *bears* up here?!"

As can be imagined, everyone was looking forward to a hearty breakfast the next morning, and the boys gathered the firewood in short order. We got a huge fire going and started frying the bacon and eggs. We hadn't had a lot of experience cooking over an open fire, so we made the fire way too hot, and we put the pan on the fire way too early. Before long, the flames jumped into the pan of bacon and eggs, and the bacon grease ignited. You should have seen the look on the boys' faces! They had all been standing around salivating at the idea of this big breakfast of bacon and eggs, and they were very hungry after all the canoeing the previous day and going to bed without any supper. Then suddenly they were looking at their bacon and eggs all charred like little black marbles in the pan. I'll never forget how disappointed the boys were. Fortunately, we had enough bacon and eggs left over that everybody did get something to eat on the second attempt when we slowed down and cooked things properly—although not the generous portions we all would have liked.

After breakfast that first morning, we proceeded on our canoe trip. Before long, we came across the home of the Boundary Water's legendary Root Beer Lady, Dorothy

Chapter Two: The Teaching Years

Molter, who lived all alone on the Isle of Pines on Knife Lake. Dorothy had lived in this spot for many years, and she was famous for selling her home-made root beer to many a thirsty traveler taking time out from their canoeing adventures to stop on her island. When we arrived at Dorothy's place, of course, the boys were very thirsty, and they all wanted root beer in the worst way, so we decided to stop and buy some. After we had enjoyed our drinks and were getting ready to launch our canoes back on the river, Dorothy took me aside and said, "I don't know if you are aware, but you've got some boys who are a little dishonest. They drank my root beer, and they didn't pay me for it." Of course, we had to clear this up and make the offending culprits "pony up" before we left.

For the most part, we all had a wonderful time on that trip. We saw lots of incredible wildlife and beautiful scenery while canoeing the pristine lakes, and the rest of our time on the water passed without further mishap.

As we headed home on the bus, however, we had another misadventure. We stopped for lunch in New Ulm, Minnesota, and the whole group ate at a local restaurant. Conducting the head count after the kids got back on the bus, I discovered that I was missing one boy. I asked the whole busload of boys, "Where's Burton? Where is he?!" I was met with silence. I said, "Come on, somebody knows where he is!" Then someone piped up and said, "The cops got him!"

It turned out that unbeknownst to me, Burton had gone into a hardware store near the restaurant and had picked up an item and stuffed it in his pocket. Well, of course, they weren't fools in that hardware store. The clerks had their eyes on Burton, and they called the cops. The cops came and picked up Burton and took him to the police station. I headed right down to the station, and there he was. I really started giving him hell. The cops were standing there watching us. I said, "You know, Burton, there are people who are in cells like the one you're standing in, who would give anything in the world to get out and be free. And you're doing everything you can to get in there. Something is wrong with this picture!" After witnessing this interaction, the cops said, "You know, we're gonna turn that kid over to you. We think you can handle him a lot better than we can and get further with him than we can." So we took Burton back with the rest of the group.

When we got back home, we heard the tragic news that the Newell FFA Chapter had lost a boy to drowning on their trip to the Ozarks. That was really devastating for everyone.

STORIES ON THE DOMESTIC FRONT

Of course, I also have some stories about events in my home life that happened during my teaching career while residing in Storm Lake (first two years), Newell (third year), and then Kingsley (fourth year).

When Von and I moved to Storm Lake, we moved into a place that was a double garage and was then converted into living quarters. It was sort of like a makeshift motel. After the war, there were a lot of housing shortages due to so many veterans settling back into civilian life, getting jobs, and needing to find housing all at once. This resulted in every conceivable space being utilized for living quarters. Our converted garage was located right across the highway from the lake. This was the first time we'd ever lived by water, so it was a whole new experience. We concluded that this was not a very safe place to raise kids, with both the lake and the highway so nearby, and we had little Dana to protect.

Basil Deegan, who was the elevator owner/operator in Sulphur Springs, got wind of our predicament, and he had a summer cottage to rent on the east side of Storm Lake, not too far from the Cobble Stone Dance Hall. So Von and I moved into the cottage with Dana. Of course, now we needed to furnish the cottage and set up housekeeping. One of the items that we had was a little washing machine that we set on a bench, and Von would wash clothes in it. It was old and outdated and left a lot to be desired. One day, we saw a notice in the newspaper that a lady had a used washing machine for sale. This washing machine had a wringer. After you would wring out the clothes as best you could, then you would hang them out on the clothesline, because we didn't have a dryer. After we bought the used machine, and I brought it home, Von was of course really itching to try it out.

I moved the washing machine in with a dolly and then proceeded to clean it up and remove the tape that was around it. When Monday morning arrived, Von intended to wash clothes like all the other ladies. I left, as usual, to teach school at Hayes.

Later that morning, the Hayes Superintendent stopped by my office. His name was Mr. Barnes, and he told me, "You'd better call home. Your wife has run into some kind of problem." It was very unusual for Von to call me at work, so I went right home. (It was only about two and half miles away). When I arrived home, there was Von, with water all over the floor. Von told me that the washing machine we had just purchased started leaking as soon as she filled it up with water. I had removed the tape when I first brought it home and had thrown the tape away. It turned out that the tape was there for a reason, and the reason was that there was a chunk of metal that had broken off the machine; once the tape was removed, it was like taking your finger out of the hole in the dyke. We cleaned up the water and taped the machine right back up. Surprisingly, it worked well for quite a while after that.

Another minor mishap Von and I had at that cottage happened during the winter of 1951 after our second daughter, Betsy, was born. The walls in our summer cottage weren't insulated, and the inner walls were only partially finished and didn't go all the way up to the ceiling. We were located on the east side of the lake, so we got the west wind blowing across the lake, and it was a bitterly cold winter that year. We had this big dissolute (oil) stove as a sort of "central heating" for the place, and we didn't know too much about how to operate it, other than that you had to put fuel oil in it and keep it lit.

We used to push Betsy's crib up close to the stove at night so she would stay warm. One winter night, Von and I were awakened by this loud "whoosh!" We jumped up to try to find out what in the world was going on. We went out and discovered that the stove had exploded and had blown soot all over Betsy in her crib. The stove had this idiosyncrasy in that it would almost entirely go out, and then there would be a little spark that would suddenly start the fire up again, and it would explode inside. When this happened, the fire would re-ignite too fast and blow the soot out the stove pipes. Betsy wasn't hurt, but she was completely covered in black soot. She didn't even wake up, and that's when we discovered that she was really a sound sleeper!

For the most part, we really enjoyed living in the cottage on Storm Lake. We had the use of a boat, and we had lots of family and friends come to visit us, especially in the summer.

The next year (1952-53), we moved to Newell, Iowa, and we lived in an upstairs apartment. The house belonged to the brother of a man, Bill Smith, who was on the school board at Sulphur Springs. Unfortunately, the lady of the house who lived down below us was suffering from stomach cancer, and she was in a lot of pain. We could often hear her moaning, and we felt very bad for her. One day we gave her quite a fright, because Betsy started to fall down the stairs that were located right above the lady's head, and I dove down after Betsy trying to catch her. Betsy was a chubby baby, and she was very active and liked to have me chase her when she was crawling around as fast as she could. She would look back at me when she was crawling away to see if I was chasing her, and then she'd get all excited and giggle. One day as I was coming around the corner, Betsy took off because she thought I was chasing her, and she fell right down the open stairway.

When I saw Betsy's little feet disappear over the edge, I made a dive and caught her by the leg about a third of the way down and held her up in the air overhead so she wouldn't hit the steps. I slid down the entire flight of stairs on my hip holding Betsy. This made quite a racket, and when I got down to the bottom, I think that the lady downstairs feared that something terrible had happened

Chapter Two: The Teaching Years

to the house, such as a truck hitting it or something catastrophic like that, and I'm sure it must have startled her quite a bit. Apparently, Betsy didn't suffer any ill effects from her tumble down the steps, because she was laughing and wanting me to chase her again within about an hour after that.

Our family left the dwelling in Newell after spending a year there and moved to Kingsley in 1954. We then rented an apartment in the upstairs of the superintendent's house.

Dana and Betsy on the front steps at Newell in the summer of 1953.

The superintendent was an older gentleman named Mr. Conners, and he and his wife lived in the lower level of the house. One thing that bothered Von was that the superintendent's wife had a cat that she was very fond of, and she would fry fish for the cat as soon as she got up in the morning. Von was pregnant at the time with our third daughter, Jayne, and the smell of frying fish first thing in the morning did not sit well with Von.

OUR FFA FEED EXPERIMENT

As I mentioned previously, I was in charge of supervising the FFA Chapters in all three of the schools where I taught.

One of the projects that my FFA Chapters got into involved an agreement with the Hanson Brothers Company of Storm Lake, as part of a fund-raising drive for the club's treasury. The Hanson brothers had a small elevator and a small feed mill and had a feeder pig sales program. They would sell farmer feeders pigs that they would truck in from Wisconsin; then they would sell the farmer on feeding their high vitamin, high fiber, high protein starter pig feed.

The pigs would start taking off and thriving nicely; however, the Hanson Brothers were not too well-versed in the intricacies of nutrition, and they had a tendency to leave their pigs on this feeding program too long. My FFA members and I noticed that the Hanson brothers' pigs started off well, but after a while, they would stall out. My FFA students decided that they could do a better job raising these feeder pigs, and they wanted to conduct a feed experiment at the same time.

Our plan was as follows: we would propose to the Hanson Brothers, along with an alternate feed company, that our FFA Chapter would buy 36 pigs, divide them into an experimental and a control group, placing the 36 pigs in two different pens—with 18 in each, feeding one set of pigs the Hanson Brothers' feeding program while feeding the other pen of pigs according to an alternate feed program from an outside company. The Hanson Brothers had already agreed to do this, and then at the end of the feeding program, when the pigs got ready for market, we would determine which feed was the most effective, that is, which had the best gains and which pigs got to market first, as well as which feeding program resulted in the lowest cost.

My FFA students went ahead and bought all 36 pigs (18 for the Hansen-fed control group and 18 for the experimental feed group), but then had difficulty finding an alternate feed company for the experimental group.

As luck would have it, we had talked to Basil Deegan, the elevator operator at Sulphur Springs, who also sold feed, and it just so happened that he sold a brand of feed that was marketed by Cargill, which was called, "Nutrena."

So I contacted Earl Raff, Nutrena Sales Manager at Sioux City, and Earl told me that their territory manager for our area was named Steve Love.

Steve sat down with me and my FFA students. We went over the program as we had planned it and asked Steve if he would be interested in furnishing feed for the other 18 pigs. Steve replied, "I'll talk it over with my boss, and then I'll get back to you." He got back to me two days later, and he said "Well, we support your experiment in theory, but . . ." And I asked, "Steve, don't you have confidence in your feed that you would be selling out here to these farmers? It would certainly be good advertising." Steve said, "That's not really what we're worried about. What we're actually worried about is how the test would be run, and we would be concerned about the possibility of a foul ball." When I asked Steve what he meant by a foul ball, he explained, "When you run feed trials like this, lots of things can happen, and we don't necessarily have control of the variables or any really good credible information on exactly what is happening to influence the results. Our feed could wind up failing through no fault of the feed or the feeder, but by some oddball thing that could happen."

I could see Steve's point, but I tried to sell him on how this would be good public relations for Nutrena. Steve agreed that it would be good advertising; nevertheless, he declined to participate in the trial. We couldn't find any other feed company close by that was interested in participating, so what we did was go ahead and make arrangements with Basil Deegan, the operator of the Sulphur Springs grain elevator. Basil then obtained information about the Nutrena feed program, and we administered the program exactly as the pamphlets instructed.

We decided to use the Nutrena feeding program as the comparator to the Hanson Brothers'—without the support of Nutrena. To start the trial, the Hanson Brothers brought the pigs out, and we gate-cut and divided the pigs into two groups. Unfortunately, some of the pigs weren't castrated, so we had to do that ourselves. We were just learning how to castrate pigs, so it was pretty hard on the pigs. In fact we had a couple of near-casualties, but the pigs ultimately pulled through. Then as they had agreed, the Hanson Brothers furnished the feed for the pigs they had sold us. We put 18 pigs on the Hanson Brothers' program, and those pigs took off like a shot. Their hair slicked up, they looked impressive, and they were healthy. We put the other pigs on Nutrena's Creep 20 for a short time, just as the feeding bulletin instructed, until they got up to a particular size. Then we noticed that a strange phenomenon was occurring. At about the weight of 35 to 40 pounds, the pigs that were on the Hanson Brother's product seemed to stall out. We told the Hanson brothers that the pigs on their feed program didn't look as if they were doing as well as the pigs on the Nutrena program after the 35–40 pound point; whereas the pigs on the Hanson-fed program had done very well and looked better than the Nutrena-fed pigs prior to that point. The Hanson Brothers didn't respond with any suggestions or solutions to our concerns, so for a while we continued the Hanson Brothers' pigs on their original program with the feed that the Hanson Brothers had bought in the first place. Soon, it got to the point where it was obvious that the Hanson Brothers'-fed pigs weren't doing nearly as well as the Nutrena-fed pigs.

We determined that we were going to have to do something to get these Hanson Brothers' pigs going, because their pigs were obviously stalling out, and the Nutrena pigs were really thriving in comparison. Of course the FFA students were going home and telling their folks about this. We were starting to get a little static from the Hanson Brothers about the difficulties we were having persuading farmers to go on to the Hanson feeding program when the pigs were bought. We decided that the only thing to do was to put all of the pigs on the Nutrena feeding program to get them ready to go to market, which we did.

Our pigs ultimately all went to market; however, the Hanson Brother's pigs were 10 to 15 days behind the Nutrena pigs in their development. The Nutrena pigs distinctly won the feeding trial, but we decided that since Nutrena had not agreed to support our experiment and furnish the feed, and since we had to go ahead and buy the feed ourselves, we would not divulge to Nutrena the results of the feeding trial. When Steve Love stopped by and asked how the project came out, we were noncommittal and simply told him the trial came out "alright." Steve knew better than to ask us more about the results, because we weren't about to tell him.

FOUR-STATE LIVESTOCK JUDGING CONTEST, SIOUX CITY
Around that time, in 1952, I was becoming involved in another important event in my teaching career, and that was the Four-State Livestock Judging Contest in Sioux City, Iowa. Four states, Iowa, Minnesota, South Dakota, and Nebraska, entered livestock judging teams that participated in this regional agricultural competition. In this contest, there were eight classes of livestock: three classes of hogs, three classes of cattle and two classes of sheep. A livestock team was made up of four boys who had livestock training from Vo Ag classes in each participating school.

Since I taught in two schools, Hayes and Sulphur Springs, I had two teams. In preparation for the contest, I had proceeded to take my students on field trips to family farms in the surrounding countryside to show them exactly what I meant when I was telling them how to "place" these animals. For the contest, the boys had to place animals in each one of those classes. For example, if they had four animals in a class, they had to place the four animals in descending ranking order with the most desirable animal first, then the second most desirable, then the third and finally, the least desirable.

Desirability was based on factors such as general health, size, and conformation based on the skeletal and muscular structures of the animal. I taught my students exactly as I'd been taught by Dr. Jim Kaiser, who had been one of my instructors at SDSU. By this time, Dr. Kaiser had left SDSU and had joined the faculty at Iowa State College in Ames, where he headed up their equine program. Since Dr. Kaiser was considered a top expert in judging, he was selected to be the master judge by the Sioux City Livestock Judging Contest.

When I heard that Dr. Kaiser was the one selected as the judge for the contest, I knew that my teams would be able to do well with judging the livestock in the various classes, because I had been training them all along according to his standards. Of course, I hadn't known ahead of time that he would be judging the contest at the time I trained my students in livestock judging, so this was a very fortunate turn of events for me and my students.

In 1952, the first year we entered in the Sioux City Livestock Judging Contest, there were 73 teams competing. Although the two teams that I took to the competition

Chapter Two: The Teaching Years

My Sulphur Springs Judging Team, which scored fourth place in the Fifth Annual FFA Livestock Judging Contest in Sioux City in 1953.

(Hayes and Sulphur Springs) both consisted of relatively young students, the boys had paid close attention to the instructions, and they did very well.

The second year, in 1953, the teams from Pender, Nebraska, and Pipestone, Minnesota, pretty well cleaned house at the competition; however, in 1954, we had just one team, which was from Sulphur Springs, and they excelled in the competition. The Sulphur Springs team took fourth place out of 97 teams, and we had the leading contestant, by the name of Wilmer Christian, who earned 782 points on eight classes of livestock out of a possible 800 points. This score resulted in winning first place in a contest involving about 500 kids! It just so happened that the prize for the first place winner was a full scholarship to

One of my students, Wilmar Christian (far left), won first prize in the Sixth Annual FFA Livestock Judging Contest in Sioux City in 1954.

Morningside College in Sioux City. Wilmer apparently remembered those days very well, because he stopped and visited Von and me at our home in Minnetonka about 35 years later. I was retired at the time. He told me that winning the judging contest and earning this scholarship at Morningside had really helped him advance in the early stages of his career.

My Teaching Position in Kingsley, Iowa

In the spring of 1954, I left Sulphur Springs for a job at Kingsley High School. I started this new position on July

1st, 1954, and continued on with that job until July 1, 1955. Because of a shortage of space at the high school, the classroom for the Kingsley Vo Ag Program was located downtown, across from the Nutrena dealership, in an abandoned garage. We fixed the garage up so that it was usable again. School buses were also kept in that garage. We took a number of field trips, and it was very handy to hop on a bus. We always had a driver to take us out to practice judging or to attend to our test corn plots. My uncle Julius Rosberg had a farm in Kingsley, and he was very receptive to running corn demonstrations where we

My daughter Betsy and I touring the Energy and Agricultural Education Center at the Chippewa Valley Technical College in Eau Claire, Wisconsin, in 2019.

were able to determine the best variety of seed corn to use in the Kingsley area.

Another big event happened to our family in 1954. Our third daughter, Jayne, was born in May of that year, just before we moved to Kingsley. The year 1954 was also memorable, because that winter we bought our first television set. It was a black and white Crosley television set. I still vividly remember bringing it home and how I averted a near catastrophe. I carefully lifted the brand new television, which was very big and heavy, out of the trunk of my car, and began backing into the house with it. Suddenly, I slipped on the kitchen floor with my cold wet shoes and fell on my back with the TV on top of me! Somehow I managed to keep the TV from breaking. I thought to myself ruefully at the time, "Everyone in the family seemed more worried about whether the TV was damaged than they were about me!"

Chapter Three:
My Career with Cargill

Have you ever had the good fortune in your life of being in just the right place at just the right time with the right ideas? I was very lucky to have the stars fall into line with my career at Cargill. My story with Cargill began when I was hired in 1955. Over the 33 ensuing years of my tenure there, I witnessed incredible progress in the cattle industry and would see Cargill become one of the world's leading integrated producers of beef, from production and marketing of cattle feed to raising and feeding cattle, to processing and providing meat to market. Cargill, Incorporated, a company specializing in agriculture, nutrition, food production, and risk management, is America's largest private company with operations spanning the globe. Cargill's mission is "helping the world thrive."

According to *Bloomberg Business Week* (June 7th, 2018), Cargill, which is one of the largest grain traders and beef packers in the world, "had a revenue of $109.7 billion in 2017 and employed about 155,000 workers . . . in offices across 70 countries." Statista.com cites Cargill as still being the largest private U.S. company by revenue in 2021, with a revenue of 134.4 billion U.S. dollars that year.

Cargill Corporate Headquarters in Wayzata, Minnesota. Courtesy of Cargill, Incorporated.

Cargill is also one of the nation's oldest companies, founded in 1865 at the end of the Civil War by William Wallace Cargill, and ownership has remained in the family ever since. Its corporate headquarters are based in Wayzata, Minnesota.

In November 2021, Cargill celebrated "Fifty years of prosperity and development in China," marking its 50th anniversary of a successful trade partnership with China at the International Import Expo in Shanghai. Also, "with fish and seafood rapidly becoming the largest source of animal protein in peoples' diets worldwide, Cargill has become a leader in the international aquaculture industry and is helping to meet global demand for sustainably farmed fish and seafood, and to satisfy the growing demand for protein into the foreseeable future."*

When I joined the Product Management staff with Cargill's Feed Division on July 1, 1955, I wasn't given any formal training by the company. That would come later. To start with, I drew upon my formative years feeding cattle on our family farm, as well as my prior knowledge, training, and experience as a vocational agriculture (Vo Ag) teacher. Particularly helpful was the experience supervising my Future Farmers of America (FFA) chapters and establishing advisory boards of local farmers in three

---
*—www.Cargill.com

farming communities in northwest Iowa. I had learned early on how critical it was to listen, and carefully assess the needs of whomever I was serving, whether that was the school district that hired me to teach their students or the community farmers with whom I was consulting. Then I would develop a targeted action plan based on the needs that were identified. This strategy of needs assessment, goal setting, and implementing follow-up action plans was a core thread that ran through everything I did in a career that evolved from Vo Ag teacher to cattle feed specialist and feedlot consultant in agribusiness.

As I look back, what I brought to Cargill had a lot to do with the proverbial lion lying in the grass on the savanna. You know the old adage, "You can learn a lot by watching"? Well, I found this to ring true in my ensuing career. I came from a family deeply rooted in agriculture. Both my maternal and paternal grandfathers, my father, most of my uncles, and my six brothers were all in the beef cattle business in some way, and of course, I had learned a lot from my family's experiences raising and feeding out cattle while growing up.

Being immersed in an agricultural background prepared me to work with the farmers I encountered during that time. I would choose the more successful members of the farming communities where I taught—those with the most to offer in terms of knowledge and experience in raising cattle. I would place these carefully selected farmers on a five-man board, and I would ask them to discuss problems they were encountering. Then *they* would tell *me* what their needs were so that I knew specifically what to focus on in providing the right information to help them. I would set up the curriculum of my adult agricultural education program according to the board's most pressing priorities. I felt that this approach helped me to become more effective in implementing the state's Vo Ag program—both with the high school/FFA and adult education components. This also helped me to become more effective as a consultant to the local farmers. My aim was to help them improve their methods—either by making their farming more efficient or more productive—or both.

PART ONE: HELPING IGNITE THE EVOLUTION OF THE ANIMAL FEED INDUSTRY

The Advent of Diethylstilbestrol : A Ground-Breaking Development in the Cattle Feed Industry
In 1954, just before I started my career with Cargill, there were some revolutionary and far-reaching developments happening in the cattle business. One of these developments involved the ground-breaking research being conducted by Dr. Wise Burroughs, a ruminant nutrition researcher and teacher at Iowa State College in Ames. On February 19, 1954, Iowa State College's Wise Burroughs, Professor of Animal Husbandry, announced at a special Iowa Cattle Feeders' Day that he had discovered a growth-promoting cattle feed additive.

According to the Iowa Beef Center at Iowa State University, Dr. Burroughs had just developed the first orally fed growth promotant and thus revolutionized protein supplementation of beef cattle.

Dr. Burroughs had discovered a way of making cattle gain weight faster on less feed by administering an orally fed additive. He had completed a research project involving diethylstilbestrol (DES), which is a synthetic, non-steroidal, growth-promoting female hormone.

Dr. Burroughs found that when DES was fed to fattening

cattle in a controlled experiment, the test cattle gained weight significantly faster and had a significantly better feed conversion. This was the first time in the history of agriculture that it was demonstrated that additive drugs could be fed orally to cattle to get a "definite measured predictable growth response." This caused quite a stir in the feed industry, because up until that time, commercial cattle feed supplement had not moved in as great a volume for Cargill, or for many other feed companies, as it had for the swine and poultry industries. This is because, with cattle, it was difficult to demonstrate that commercial feed did a better job than just plain vegetable oil meal in successfully balancing a ration. At that time, in an effort to successfully balance rations, many of the cattle on the range were fed cottonseed meal, and cattle in feedlots were fed mostly soybean and linseed oil meal as a protein supplement. Many feedlot cattle were able to get their protein from other natural sources without the benefit of commercial beef feed and supplements, but the gains were definitely much slower and less profitable.*

Also, up until that time, in most cases in Iowa, cattle had been raised through many diversified (small, self-contained, nonspecialized) farming operations, which didn't require a lot of extra labor, other than storing up

---

*—DES was eventually banned in 1979.

feed and hay for the animals during the off season. Most of these diversified farmers did not have a large number of cattle; they tended to have 10 to 20 head. They would keep the female calves (heifers), and the heifers would become part of their breeding herd as the older cows were culled out and sent to market. The male calves (steers), would be either fed to market size or sold as feeder cattle.

Getting Hired and Starting out with Cargill

Suddenly, with the advent of DES, there was a realization that technology could make feeding cattle more efficient. Also, having effective additives meant that commercial cattle feed was going to become much more of a saleable commodity. In light of these important new research developments in the cattle business, the Feed Division of Cargill decided that they needed to gear up and get ready to market much more commercial cattle feed. Cargill made it known that they were looking for an individual who could help them establish beef product sales for the company.

Within Cargill, when I first joined the company, there was a number of individuals who were experienced in and knowledgeable about raising hogs, and there were also a number of people who knew a lot about poultry products and the problems associated with poultry production, especially in the area of laying hens and raising baby chicks. Cargill had tended to struggle in the cattle sector, however, and Cargill's salesforce had not moved a high volume of cattle feed (other than plain old oil meal). Up to that time, no company, including Cargill, had figured out the science behind cattle feed or how to sell it. The company didn't have very many people who knew much in general about the cattle industry or in particular about cattle feed, so Cargill was on the look-out to hire someone who was familiar with the various aspects of raising and feeding cattle.

As luck would have it, I had established some valuable connections during my college years and during my years as a Vo Ag teacher. Two of these contacts, Ray Switzer and Warren Engelland, had been in my 1951 graduating class at SDSU, and both of these men ended up being key to my future employment at Cargill. Ray was a well-known livestock radio announcer who had moved to take a new job at the Sioux City Stockyards, in Iowa, with a commission company called Gehan and Sons. Warren had gone to work for Cargill as a product manager for hog feed. From their time together at SDSU, Warren knew that Ray was a highly regarded expert as far as the basics of the cattle industry was concerned, so he recommended that Cargill try to recruit Ray for its new position of Beef Product Manager. Consequently, Ray was invited to Minneapolis to interview for this job opening. When Gehan found out that Cargill was interested in Ray, it made him a counteroffer of a job that included part ownership in their company.

This of course, appealed immensely to Ray, who was very knowledgeable about the cattle business around Sioux City, as well as about the business of bringing livestock into the Sioux City stockyards and selling fat cattle and buying feeder cattle in that market. Although interested in Cargill, Ray ultimately decided to stay with Gehan and become part owner.

Meanwhile, Cargill had been planning on hiring Ray, and it was a shock to them when they realized that their number one candidate was not going to accept their offer. So Warren asked Ray who else he thought would be a good prospect for the job. Ray said, "Well there's this Vo Ag instructor from northwest Iowa, Jim McDougall, whom we both know. I've seen Jim bring in his livestock judging teams. In fact, one of his boys won a major scholarship for taking first place in the last Sioux City livestock judging contest. Jim is from a large cattle raising family and knows quite a lot about cattle. I'd suggest you take a look at him."

Cargill followed up on Ray's suggestion, and in early spring of 1955, I was invited to Minneapolis to interview with Frank Berry, who was in charge of advertising and promotion of the Feed Division of Cargill. I borrowed my dad's car, a brand new Chevy, and drove from Le Mars to Minneapolis on a Friday evening in early June. Bud Harder, the coach from Kingsley High School, where I was teaching at the time, accompanied me. We stayed that night at the Nicollet Hotel at the north end of Nicollet Avenue. The next morning, I went over to the Cargill Office, which at that time was located in the Flour Exchange Building across the street from the Grain Exchange Building. The interview took place Saturday morning. Afterward, Frank took me to Charley's Café for lunch and then showed me around Minneapolis a bit.

Before meeting with Frank, the main part of Minneapolis that I had seen was down Nicollet Avenue from my hotel. This happened to be a pretty rough neighborhood at that time. I recall that Frank had asked me, "Well, what do you think of our town?" I replied, "Well, Frank, I looked out the window last night and heard all this commotion, and it turned out to be just a bunch of drunks stumbling around and getting into fights. Frankly, I don't think very much of this part of your town." Frank seemed shocked that I wasn't more impressed with Minneapolis, at least not at first glance.

As it turned out, Frank offered me the job with Cargill. I was hired to go to work on July 1st, 1955, and my primary responsibility was to lead the marketing of Cargill's beef products. My title at that time was listed as

Beef Feed Product Manager or Cattle Feed Product Manager.

Understanding the unique nature of a ruminant's stomach was one of the primary strengths that I brought to Cargill right from the start of my career and was key to the contributions I would end up making down the road, including being instrumental in developing the Prescription Feeding Program and the Cargill Feedlot System. Both of these systems were vitally important factors in balancing the ruminant's ration.*

I had studied extensively about the unique features of bovine digestion during my college training and had started to apply this knowledge during my years teaching Vo Ag. It didn't take me long to realize how critical this knowledge would become in my career as Beef Feed Product Manager with Cargill.

During my initial interview with Frank Berry, upon joining Cargill, I had shared my thoughts about

Clipping from the Minneapolis Morning Tribune announcing my joining Nutrena, Cargill in 1955.

---

*—A ration is defined as a fixed allowance of total feed for an animal to eat in one day.

increasing Cargill's feed business, including my ideas about the importance of balanced rations. One of the primary considerations that I went over with Frank was the importance of demonstrating how the stomach of a cow operates so differently than simple-stomached animals. It is a real distinct phenomenon. At that time, most people, including even many of those within the cattle feed business, did not understand the complexity of the bovine digestive system—that the cow's stomach has four compartments, and that these compartments operated together to utilize the necessary bacteria to help the cattle digest their feed.

The crux of the issue in the cattle feed industry is this: If you don't know what you are doing ration-wise with cattle or why you are doing it, you can kill them. Some of the farmer feeders found that out the hard way. Because of the cow's complex digestive system, if you put too much energy into the rumen too quickly, when the cattle are first going on feed in the feedlot, and are very hungry, they can develop lactic acidosis. If they ingest too much energy too fast, a number of bad things can happen. The cattle can bloat up and even die. Another dire consequence is that they might become crippled. If they are fortunate, they might recover, but their growth is usually impaired after that.

This underscores the importance of providing the right ration at the right time in the feeding process. The composition of the ration would change as the animal finishes the fattening period. Ruminant bacteria was another important consideration that had to be factored in when developing an optimal feeding program in cattle.

Concept of the Balanced Ration

The balanced ration was the cornerstone of our operation in the Beef Development Department of Cargill. I felt so strongly about the importance of conveying an understanding of the cattle's digestive system, that very early on in my career with Cargill, I decided to have a physical model made of a cow's stomach for demonstration purposes. To accomplish this, in 1958-59, I enlisted the help of Dr. Wes Nelson, Director of Animal Research, together with beef research specialists at the University of Minnesota, to produce this model.

We had the stomach of a 700-pound yearling cleaned and dried out and then coated with plastic. Then we cut small window-like openings with hinged lids attached in each of the four sections of the cow's stomach so that each section could be viewed. I ended up using this model for demonstration purposes with the salesforce numerous times during my years with the Cargill Sales Force, with many prospects and customers, and at one of the National Cattlemen's Conventions.

In the late 1950s, we used an actual cow's stomach, preserved in resin, to demonstrate how cattle digest feed. Courtesy of Cargill, Incorporated.

Evolution in Marketing Strategies

At the time I joined Cargill in 1955, some major industry changes were already in the air. The old method of selling feed, with radio advertising, store posters, and gimmicks, was no longer getting the job done. Many Cargill Feed Division personnel, including Frank Berry, were aware of this and were scrambling to start making the changes that would help Cargill stay competitive and continue to grow its business. These changes involved the Cargill salesforce and its aim to capture and maintain its market share of the beef business. Up until the mid-1950s, Cargill's salesforce, for the most part, was an established group of men in a rather mature, stagnant industry. This salesforce had been trained to service their market through a large number of small individual dealerships, and many of Cargill's sales reps moved a relatively small amount of their signature Nutrena brand feed products. Cargill had a system of territory managers who were in charge of servicing certain feed store dealers. These dealers were set up close enough together to make it handy and convenient for farmers to come in to the feed store or a feed mill, purchase their feed, and haul it out by themselves.

Nutrena, a company acquired by Cargill in 1945, was the flagship retail brand of Cargill that specialized in animal nutrition research and science, animal feed products and marketing innovations.* Initially, one of the primary Nutrena products sold was feed for baby chicks, and when I

---

*— www.Cargill.com

Chapter Three: My Career with Cargill

Ad for Nutrena Feeds in the Le Mars, Iowa Daily Sentinal; July 17, 1961. Courtesy of Cargill, Incorporated.

started out working for Cargill, much of the chick feed was sold in either 50 pound paper bags or 100 pound cloth bags. The farmers bought it as they needed it, usually around late February or early March of each year, when the baby chicks were hatched. The other type of feed that moved in volume was the pig starter feed, Nutrena's Creep-20, plus protein supplements such as Shoat 40 Concentrate for hogs being fattened for sale on the market.

Cargill's territory managers serviced their dealers by presenting co-op ads with radio and local newspapers, plus putting up posters in their dealers' stores. The territory managers would also train the dealers on how to use targeted strategies in making face-to-face field sales calls on the swine producers.*

In those days, for the most part, Cargill's salesforce avoided direct sales contacts with large cattle producers or big dairy operators, because the sales representatives knew very little about beef and dairy animals' special needs and what to recommend for feeding programs and why. After my discussions with Frank Berry and watching the sales reps operating at dealerships, it became clear to me just how daunting a task lay ahead of me. I realized that Cargill didn't yet have a well-developed cattle feed program. The salesmen who were operating in the

---

*—"Sales points to close sales" is a term which refers to explaining the benefits of the purchase, such as that of balancing the ration.

feed companies at the time were sometimes considered to be unscrupulous, and many of the farmers didn't necessarily trust them. Their reputation wasn't very good on the larger beef farms. During my initial job interview with Frank, I had commented that Cargill had a big job to do. I said, "Your people don't know much about ruminants, including how they digest their feed and all that that entails." Frank agreed with me. He said, "Yes, feeding cattle is different, but we think there is going to be a lot of business coming down the pike very soon, so we need to get ready to handle it."

As I began my new job with Cargill, I was about to learn many important lessons about what it would take to move feed products more successfully and efficiently in larger volume, from feed sold in sacks to bulk feed by the truckloads. As I learned more about Cargill's sales promotion efforts for swine and poultry products, I decided that I would try to avoid repeating previous mistakes while teaching Cargill's salesforce to branch out into the selling of beef and dairy products. The challenges that lay ahead of me were three-fold: educating myself and my salesforce about designing the best product for cattle feeders based on knowing the animal and how it digests the feed; testing the product and working out the bugs before launching the product; and then marketing the product more successfully to farmers and beef producers. I also learned the importance of developing trust with the farmers and going out of my way to connect with both prospective and current customers by visiting them on their own turf.

When I came on board with Cargill in the mid-1950s, the salesforce was in the midst of planning its "Fifty Grand" Egg Feed Campaign. This campaign wound up guaranteeing the chicken feeders a specific egg increase over their previous feeding program. It also involved changes in our chicken feed production system, which required the company to inject liquid fat directly into the feed mix. Both the specific egg increase guarantee and the injection of liquid fat into the feed resulted in unforeseen difficulties that definitely had some negative consequences, which should have been anticipated.

This experience taught me that when our company came up with new products and programs, it was imperative that our product management team first test them thoroughly prior to launching them in the field. Our small swine and poultry testing facility at Pleasant Hill, Missouri, could not give us the kind of answers we needed. The lessons we learned concerning the Fifty Grand Egg Feed Campaign made it much easier to convince our management team that we needed to have a larger and more advanced research center nearby. We needed a research operation that would ensure that products and programs would work as expected before we presented them to our salesforce to promote in the field. The realization of the importance of research testing was developing across the industry, including with many of our competitors, not just at Cargill.

Development of Regional Feeder Meetings

Most of my first year with Cargill in 1955 was spent holding a series of meetings with a variety of dealers in Nutrena's northern region. This included regional feeder meetings in central Illinois, Iowa, and Nebraska, which had a nucleus of a few truly exceptional salespeople. This area had Cargill dealerships that competed with Kent Feeds and had some outstanding salesmen who were ambitious and eager to learn as much as possible about successful cattle feeding operations. In the fall of each year, some of these top sales representatives, including four men, Bob Gladson, Don Palmer, Al Garrison and Chuck Nicklas, helped their dealers put on meetings for their cattle feeder customers, providing them with a big evening meal in a church hall or community center, followed by a sales presentation and announcing the coming year's feed price contracts (booking prices) for the fall and winter sales periods.

During my tenure with Cargill, our Feed Division was organized into regional groups of five to ten territory managers who reported to one district sales manager. Over time, the territory managers urged their district sales managers to have a representative from the Feed Division at Cargill Headquarters to speak at sales presentations. On many occasions, I was sent by Headquarters to give general marketing advice, as well as to answer the sales managers' questions about particular problems they were facing with feeding cattle at any given time and to provide reasons why they should purchase Nutrena feed. Of course, this included explaining the digestive system of ruminants, as well as telling the Rumalife story and explaining what Rumalife contributed to the balanced ration. Rumalife was Cargill's unique combination of micro-ingredients put into

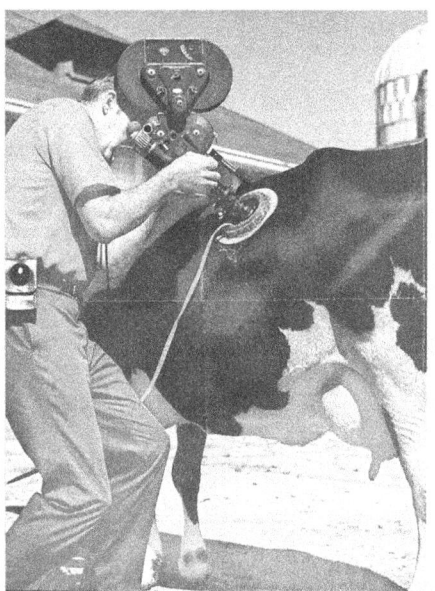

Meet Suzie.
Study of her inside digestion helps Nutrena develop special
RUMALIFE

- Special blend of ingredients aids digestion of roughage
- Helps produce milk economically
- Helps reduce feed costs
- Helps keep cows in good flesh
- ...the plus in all Nutrena dairy and beef Feeds

Nutrena Feeds

Advertisement featuring Nutrena's Rumalife product. Courtesy of Cargill, Incorporated.

their supplement to enhance the ruminant bacterial activity; in other words, providing the necessary nutrients in the proper amounts and combinations at the right time in the feeding program for Nutrena's cattle feed supplement to work optimally along with the bacteria in the cow's stomach.

This particular group of territory managers was saying, "We heard about this 'new Nutrena Beef guy,' who is supposed to be taking care of cattle feed products in Minneapolis, and maybe we can get him out here to speak to our feeders." So since I was the "new Nutrena guy," I got into a circuit every fall where I went out and helped the salesforce hold a regional cattle feeder meeting. That is how I got acquainted with different interested salesmen and a lot of their more successful cattle feeders throughout the Midwest, especially in Illinois and Iowa, during the first four years that I worked with Cargill.

The timing of the regional cattle feeder meetings was critical. These meetings were usually held at the completion of the harvest season and corresponded with the movement of feeder cattle into the cattle feeder's operation in the fall of each year. Because of the demand for face-to-face meeting contact with our territory managers and dealers, and with so many cattle feeders throughout the Midwest needing our consultation services at the same time, we decided to try to become more efficient and to reach more prospects and customers all at once. Our territory managers' general intent was to start holding two or three larger regional farmer feeder meetings each fall according to where the grain typically ripened first and then follow the progression of the grain harvest the best we could, thus eliminating the need for a proliferation of individual small feeder meetings, which had been the practice previously.

In those larger, expanded regional feeder meetings, which involved dealers throughout the area, the organizers would have staff or volunteers check in the participants and hand out their nametags and other materials. Then we'd start the meeting and have a presentation on a featured topic based on the identified concerns of that season, which usually pertained to feeding incoming cattle and promoting the cattle's optimum health through such procedures as vaccinations and antibiotics.

As Cargill's Beef Specialist, I would follow the guest speaker and talk about the importance of balancing rations or introduce new Nutrena feeding products. Then we'd break for lunch. We'd cook some beef, typically a top sirloin butt, often starting the night before, in the special Cargill cooker. The participants would come through the buffet line and help themselves to sliced beef, potato salad, etc. Right after lunch, the participants would go from booth to booth, trade-show style. These booths featured different

Nutrena-brand additive-products such as dewormer, and antibiotic concentrates, and paired Nutrena's salesmen with pharmaceutical company representatives, who were promoting their products and offering specials. At the booths, we would book the feeders' beef supplement supply for the coming season and sell specialized feeding products to start the cattle. This approach marked the beginning of a successful marketing strategy that Cargill

Explaining market factors as Cargill's Beef Specialist in the late 1950s. Courtesy of Cargill, Incorporated.

expanded on and implemented on a company-wide basis over the next decade or so in places where there was considerable beef feed potential.

The Prescription Feeding Program

As new research and technology breakthroughs were revolutionizing the cattle feed industry in the 1950s and 60s, new developments in turn started to pick up speed with cattle feed marketing for Cargill. As more of our territory managers and sales representatives were able to convince larger commercial cattle feeders to try Cargill's program, we needed to get these larger cattle feeders to put their cattle on a well-balanced ration. This was one of my primary challenges when I came on board with Cargill: to help the company, and our new customers, utilize cutting-edge advances in new research and technology and apply them to the management of feeding cattle.

This brings me to one of my key contributions to Cargill, which was the development of the Prescription Feeding Program.*

Cargill's Prescription Cattle Feeding Program turned out to be truly revolutionary. The essence of the program

---

*— The Prescription Feeding Program started with beef cattle, but down the road we further developed it and utilized it with dairy cattle and with other ruminants, such as sheep and also with horses.

Chapter Three: My Career with Cargill

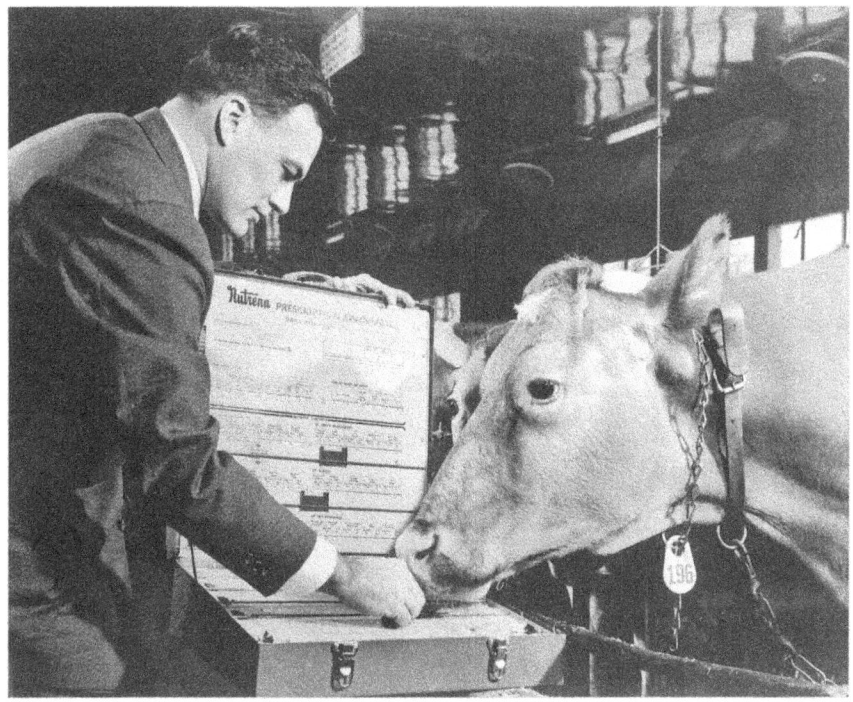

Promoting the Nutrena Prescription Calculator in the 1950s. Courtesy of Cargill, Incorporated.

was to correctly balance the ration for optimum feeding of beef cattle and to present the right rations for feeding the cattle at the proper time in the most effective way. In a nutshell, prescription feeding involves providing the necessary amount of three vital components of the ration: 1) Energy (mega-cals); 2) Roughage (fiber); and 3) The correct supplementation of protein, vitamins, and minerals.

Energy includes the nutritional components contributing to fattening the animal and modulating the animal's body temperature, and can be found in a variety of sources, including protein, grain, roughage (hay or silage), fiber, and by-products. The advent of prescription feeding had a tremendous impact, because it helped the feeders get their cattle to convert more pounds of marketable beef from the feeders' homegrown feed ingredients. Prescription feeding got the farmer to plan ahead and make more economical marketing decisions by incorporating by-products into the ration.

In many cases, before the mid-50s, if a prospect or customer wanted to talk about cattle feeding rations, the feed salesman changed the subject, because he didn't always know enough about a balanced ration or why it was important and what were the actual benefits. Even if he knew it was important, he often didn't know how to create a balanced ration. He didn't want to talk about what he didn't fully understand. In addition, the salesmen found that many cattlemen could be intimidating. The cattle feeders often thought of themselves as a cut above hog raisers and chicken raisers and other diversified farmers.

If the cattle feeders sensed that the salesman didn't know what he was talking about or didn't have much to offer, they would let him know by asking, "How many cattle have you fed, son?," and then would dismiss anything further the salesman had to say.

With the advent of Cargill's prescription feeding program, the door opened to more direct sales opportunities, and it made our sales people want to seek out the cattle feeder rather than accidentally stumble onto one and then get intimidated by him. This prescription feeding system developed by Cargill was a real game changer. It was the first effort that any sizeable feed company had made to help the farmer feeder other than sending in some "so-called consultant" to add to the confusion rather than actually helping the farmer feeders to balance their rations. With many cattle feeders, prescription feeding was a door opener, but more importantly in the overall scheme of things, it helped train Cargill's salesforce on how to make the right recommendations about use of our feed products.

In helping to balance the rations, prescription feeding also provided a way for the farmer feeder to get more value out of his feedstuffs and thus more gain from the feed provided to the animal. This represented a revolutionary breakthrough by Cargill to introduce and implement a way for the cattle farmer to take advantage of cutting-edge research improvements in the industry.

In the fall of each year, starting in the mid-1950s, as the feeder cattle were coming into the larger commercial feedlots, more and more of our ambitious sales people started calling on the more successful cattle feeders. It was then that the larger feeders saw the real benefits of feeding a well-balanced ration rather than our competitors' old line of "just feed the cattle two pounds a day of our 'Brand X' supplement, along with whatever grain or roughage you have on hand, in the amounts you want to feed, and they will do just fine." Even our larger competitors sold their beef supplements that way. The Cargill salesforce started to gain on the competition by providing a balanced ration using the feeders' grain and roughage, plus the best-suited Nutrena beef supplement, in just the right amounts. Our salespeople grew more competent and confident as it became evident that the animals on our balanced rations were out-performing the competition's. Also, because Nutrena's balanced rations had the correct amount of the necessary supplement, our feed program in many cases cost less per pound of ration and consequently resulted in reduced cost of gain.

There were other important components to Cargill's Prescription Feeding Program, besides the concept of a balanced ration, such as bunk management and improved health maintenance. Bunk management involves the presentation of feed in an optimal manner to the cattle. This entails several factors, such as providing the right amount of feed at the right time of day and providing the right amount of space so that all of the animals can access the feed. The health maintenance program involved factors such as vaccinations, deworming, dehorning, and detecting and treating illnesses, in addition to providing a healthy diet.

PRESCRIPTION FEEDING EXPANDS

As an increasing number of Cargill cattle feed field representatives, who were in many cases the territory managers, dealers or hired field salesmen (also known as country salesmen), started to call me to have their customers' rations balanced and checked, I faced a new challenge. The field representative would contact me and say, "I'm calling on a cattle feeder who is ready to set up his feeding program—what's the best way to introduce Cargill's products to him?" This rapidly growing volume of customers meant that, in many cases, I had to balance the ration and then get the calculated ration values back out to our salesforce to deliver them to the farmer feeders in a timely manner. This of course proved to be quite complicated and time-consuming.

At that time, I was using the company's Friden Electronic Calculators to help me compute the rations, which was considered advanced technology for its time. To speed up the process, I started to improvise ways to balance the rations by constructing sets of handmade charts in advance. These charts showed the amount of digestible protein (Total Digestible Nutrients—TDN) that was contained in each pound of ration, e.g., 1 pound, 2 pounds, 3 pounds or 20 pounds etc. of grain, plus the same kind of charts for the various roughages, (hay and silage), plus the fractional amounts of various Nutrena supplements.

Moisture content in the various feeds was also a major factor to consider in the calculations.

Over time, with the help of these rudimentary prescription feeding charts, I was able to better explain what would happen if a ration was not balanced. If you had almost everything, but you didn't include a certain important ingredient, then the ration wasn't going to perform optimally up to the anticipated point, and you were going to waste feed and require more ration per pound of gain. This concept was meaningful to the prospects or customers, and it was something they could easily understand.

I kept a set of these charts in my desk drawer, so that when someone called in, I would get the charts out, and I would put in the kind of cattle the feeder had and the nutrient requirements for the cattle at their particular stage of development. I would also find out what specific ingredients the feeder was planning to feed the cattle, as well as which Nutrena product was optimal, and then work all these factors into a balanced set of rations to be fed in the recommended amounts at the proper time. Although the charts helped quite a bit, they still were not efficient enough to keep up with the increasing demand that arose in helping the sales representatives in the field to figure out the balanced ration for the many farmer feeders they served. As the volume of requests continued to increase, it became more and more evident that there was a need for a still more efficient way to administer the Prescription Feeding Program.

Keep in mind, the farmer feeder was dealing with ever-changing feed requirements, because the cattle would keep growing in size and increasing their feed requirements. The farmer would normally purchase yearling feeder cattle at about 650 pounds, and they would feed them up to the 1000-1500 pound range until they were fat and ready for market.

I vividly recall a conversation I had around 1957 or 1958 with Ralph Grier, Feed Division Sales Training Director, when he came by and asked, "What is this I hear about you balancing rations for our field representatives?" I explained, "Well yes. Our guys run into these difficult situations involving attempting to balance a ration that they are not comfortable with. They aren't sure just how to go about it, so they call me up on the phone and ask me, and I'm just trying to help them do their job."

Ralph replied, "Well that's not a real efficient way time-wise to help them." I said, "It takes too long for me to figure out a balanced ration on a Friden calculator each time, so consequently I have the calculations all worked out in advance in chart form in terms of the ingredients of the feedstuffs. Then I am ready for the questions the salesmen might ask me. I use those charts, and it really speeds up the process." Ralph ended up saying, "Let's get those charts out into the field." That really made a lot of sense. After my talk with Ralph, I put the charts together and made them into a hand-held flip chart book that was more portable for use in the field.

APPLYING PRESCRIPTION FEEDING TO LARGER OPERATIONS
The needs of the farmer feeder drove the whole approach of prescription feeding. This was the most important emphasis of our marketing approach. As we were working toward prescription feeding, we were telling the farmer feeder how many pounds of feed to provide per day of this or that ingredient to include in the balanced ration. With the advent of the more portable prescription feeding devices, such as the flip chart and slide rule formats, our sales representative could bring the information on prescription feeding directly to the cattle feeder. He could dial in the characteristics of the farmer feeder's cattle and their current feed program, and the prescription calculator would tell the farmer what other feed ingredients, in exactly what amounts, should be added to optimize the cattles' daily diet. He could also inform the feeders of the consequences of not providing the proper ingredients at the right time.

This made quite an impression on the cattle feeder. Prior to this, most feeders were just roughly guessing. Bringing the prescription feeding charts into the field impressed

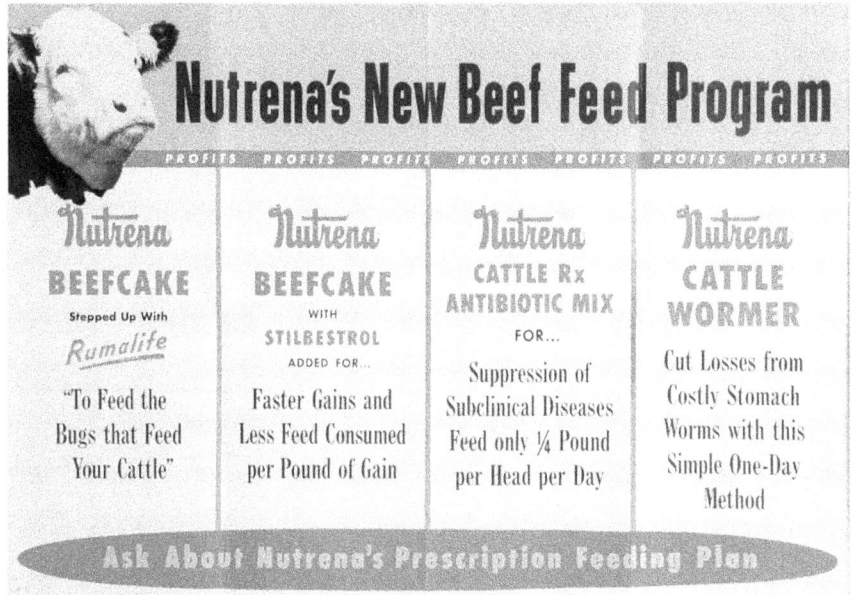

Nutrena's Beef Feed Programs. Courtesy of Cargill, Incorporated.

upon the feeders the importance of weighing the various ingredients into a balanced feed ration. The farmer feeders realized that they needed to get more precise about the individual ingredients in their feeding programs. Now suddenly for many of the farmer feeders, the way to become more precise was to have a feeder wagon that weighed the ingredients. That investment often opened the door for him to become a larger operation. This in turn prompted substantial growth in Cargill's business, as well as growth in the beef industry in general.

The Prescription Feeding Program evolved through a series of different formats. The concept originated in charts

Nutrena Farm Book of Management and Feeding. Courtesy of Cargill, Incorporated.

Chapter Three: My Career with Cargill

THE RUMEN
The most important machine you own

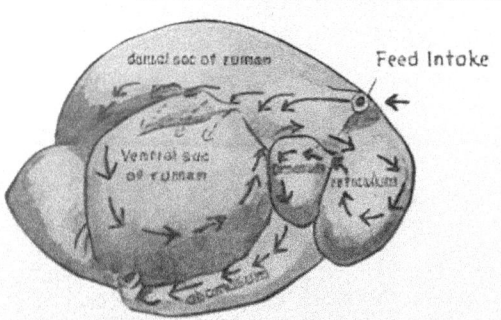

Operating Instructions
for this machine

Horse Power: About 1500 billion bacteria per cubic inch when at peak performance. Gains become less efficient as bacteria population is reduced.

Life Expectancy: Bacteria live about 24 hours. They must constantly multiply and reproduce.

Performance: Bacteria break down the fiberous roughage leaving a pulp that is easily digested by the animals.

True Value: Bacteria pass from the rumen with the partially digested roughage and grain. They are digested and absorbed by the animal. Their bodies supply protein and B vitamins.

Special Fuel: Rumen bacteria require a **constant** and even flow of "fuel". Nitrogen and minerals for reproduction and growth. Quick energy for work.

CATTLE — 1

Sample inside page of Nutrena Farm Book–The Rumen. Courtesy of Cargill, Incorporated.

RUMALIFE

A special bacteria fuel that supplies

Nitrogen: Quickly available nitrogen from urea. Slower available nitrogen from vegetable oil meals.

Molasses: Quick energy so bacteria start breaking down roughage immediately. **Controlled, even supply important.**

Trace Minerals: Ruminants must have **constant, even supply** of iron, copper, manganese, iodine, cobalt, potassium and sulphur. Used to manufacture complete proteins and B vitamins in their bodies.

Calcium: Used by the bacteria and as a direct source of calcium for the beef animal's body. Bacteria will perish in a highly acid rumen. Calcium assists in maintaining a "sweet" rumen.

Phosphorus: Maintenance and growth of bones, helps maintain the appetite and guards against phosphorus deficiency.

Vitamin A: Guards against swollen hocks, night blindness, failure to breed and infections.

Vitamin D: Anti-ricket vitamin needed by animal to properly utilize calcium and phosphorus.

CATTLE — 2

Rumalife

Sample page of Nutrena Farm Book—Rumalife. Courtesy of Cargill, Incorporated.

NUTRENA BEEFCAKE PRESCRIPTION

900 lb · 2 yr old

	Amount of Feed per Animal	Total Digestible Protein	Total Digestible Nutrients

Step 1. DAILY REQUIREMENTS OF YOUR CATTLE ARE (Pages 14 to 16): 26 lbs. 1.6 lbs. 16 lbs.

YOUR BALANCED RATION SHOULD CONTAIN

Step 2. Hay-good   4 lbs.   .42 lbs.   2.01 lbs.
Roughage (Pages 18 to 25)

_____ lbs.   _____ lbs.   / lbs.
Roughage (Pages 18 to 25)

Step 3. Ear Corn   18 lbs.   .95 lbs.   13.17 lbs.
Grain (Pages 26 and 27)

_____ lbs.   _____ lbs.   _____ lbs.
Grain (Pages 26 and 27)

Step 4. 22   1½ lbs.   .29 lbs.   .81 lbs.
Beefcake (Pages 31 and 32)

Step 5. TOTAL IN YOUR BALANCED RATION   23½ lbs.   16.6 lbs.   15.99 lbs.

- The totals in Step 5 should equal or exceed the Daily Requirements in Step 1.
- In this Balanced Ration, adequate amounts of Vitamin A, Vitamin D, Calcium, Phosphorus, Sulphur, Iron, Cobalt, Copper, Manganese and Iodine are supplied by the Rumalife in Nutrena Beefcake.

_____ lbs. Beefcake for 1 animal X _____

NX-93C   head = _____ total lbs. per day.

Sample prescription for Nutrena Beefcake. Courtesy of Cargill, Incorporated.

spread out over my desk. Then there was a "Flip Chart" version, followed by the Prescription Calculator "briefcase" apparatus. The case weighed about 25 pounds and was very bulky. We eventually converted the Prescription Calculator briefcase version into a more portable "slide rule" format—the sales representatives would complain that the briefcase version of the Prescription Calculator was too bulky to carry out in the field and would catch on their pants and snag them.

The basic concept behind the various versions of the Prescription Calculator was the same. In all the devices, you entered data in terms of weight of the cattle, along

Prescription Feeding Calculator in briefcase format. Courtesy of Cargill, Incorporated.

Chapter Three: My Career with Cargill

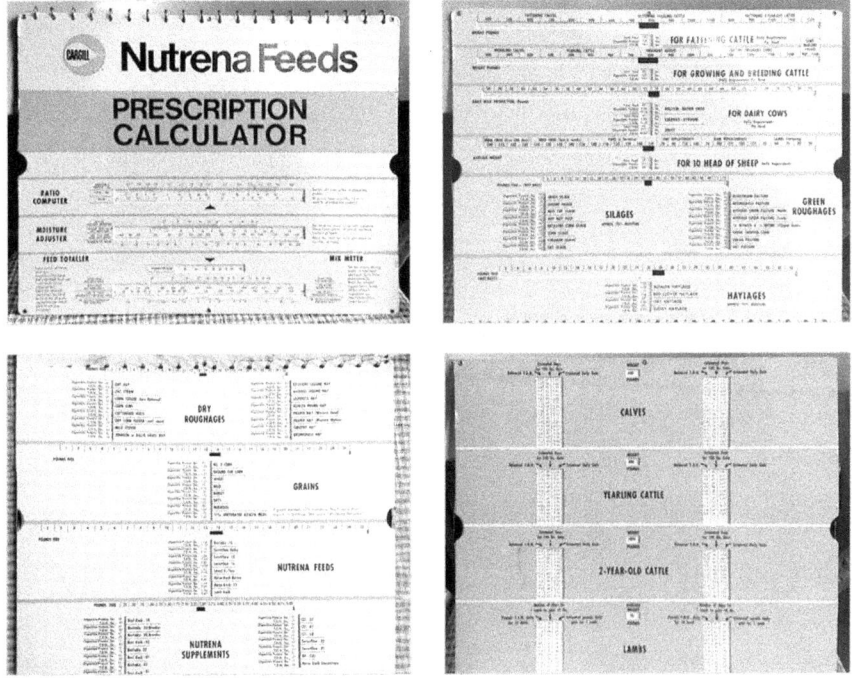

Smaller, more portable version of the Prescription Feeding Calculator for use out in the field. Courtesy of Cargill, Incorporated.

with the grain and supplement according to your targeted objectives. You could change prescriptions every 100 pounds of gain or so. The calculator indicated the designated amount of each ingredient going into the ration for the targeted objective. If you were going from 500 to 600, 600 to 700 pounds that the cattle weighed, the ration requirements changed. A lot of cattle feeders fed the same ration all the way through the feeding period; however, that is not the most efficient way to do it, and prescription feeding proved that.

Another major benefit was that prescription feeding gave a more accurate picture of the costs of gain and break-even prices to the feeder, and this helped tremendously with decision-making in purchasing and marketing.

The Cargill Feedlot System

In the early 1960s, certain high performing members of the Cargill salesforce began to experience more and more success with the Prescription Feeding Program, and over time this approach gradually developed into what became known as The Cargill Feedlot System (CFS). CFS essentially represented the marriage between the Prescription Feeding Program and computerized tools. With the evolution of the computer, the tools used to calculate rations changed as well. In fact, Cargill was the first company to calculate feed formulation completely by computer, shortly after acquiring the IBM 650 in 1957. This was described as "an industry turning point that gave a pricing advantage to customers, and a new competitive edge to Cargill."*

This is how the Cargill Feedlot System worked: The field salesforce would send in the components of the farmers' feeding program, along with their prices, to my

---

*— "Nature & Technology Unite in the Computer Age." www.Cargill.com

Chapter Three: My Career with Cargill

Presenting on the Cargill Feedlot System in the Nutrena Feeds booth at a cattle feed trade show. Courtesy of Cargill, Incorporated.

office, and I would work with my secretaries and technicians at the Central Office where the macro-computer was located. We would input the data which included the feedstuffs the farmer had available, along with the roughage and supplement values, and any other variables needing to be factored in, such as the moisture content of the components. The technician would then run the components through the computer and would configure four rations for the farmer feeder: a starting ration, two interim rations, and a finishing ration, to follow the cattle as they matured and gained weight. The field specialist would find the missing information about the components and get back to the farmer feeder. The technicians could adjust the ration accordingly. This could be a complicated procedure.

The information provided by the computer was given in percentages per 100 pounds. The computer would indicate the percent of the grain to put in the ration, as well as the percent of the Nutrena supplement to put in. Then we would take those rations and give the field representative back what we call mill sheets. The mill sheets were graduated to indicate how much of each ingredient to put into the ration. They were designed to be taken out with the feed wagon to weigh the various ingredients in a precise manner for the various types of cattle and the various stages of their growth. A mill sheet had all the rations broken down into 100, 500 and 1,000 pound units of ration and so forth. In essence, we were giving the farmer feeder more useful information than most other feedlot consultants were providing.

Revising Feedlot Objectives

In the early 1960's, Pete McVay, Executive Vice President of Cargill, contacted me and said he felt there was a great potential market for Cargill feed products in the large feedlots in Kansas, where he was from. Pete had recently been promoted, and we were flying back together from a meeting on hog production in Green Bay, Wisconsin. On that flight, he told me that he thought the future of the cattle feeding business was to be found in the large feedlots, and he wanted our salesforce to concentrate on this market. At the time, most of these feedlots were working with independent consultants, and these consultants regarded Cargill as a competitor. This new undertaking played a substantial role in refining the Cargill Feedlot System, bringing cattle feeding to a whole new level of sophistication. I was given the assignment of assembling and leading a group of specialists known as the Cargill Feedlot Group, with the mission of helping to establish Cargill products in the large commercial cattle feedlots.

This is how our feedlot specialists sometimes worked with the large feedlot operators in the early stages of the Cargill Feedlot System: The farmer feeder typically wasn't all that sophisticated. We started out at a pretty basic level, helping this farmer who just wanted to get his cattle fed. He was typically feeding grain and roughage and approximately two pounds of supplement in the cattle's ration daily. We helped refine what he was doing. Our territory managers and field representatives/country salesmen would go out with the farmer into the field where the cattle were fed. They'd obtain the feeding ingredients, and they'd send the information to our team at the Central Office. We would identify the protein and moisture levels and everything about that silage or haylage or wet corn or distiller's byproducts, as well as the price of the component ingredients, to come up with the cost of the total ration. Then we would input the data into the computer, and we would program the computer to calculate the ration to the mega cal* level. We had it all figured out as to where the cattle should start out, and when we would need to move the cattle up to higher energy rations. We would print these readings out for the cattle feeder.

Cargill's feedlot specialists teamed up with the local feedlot managers to make a lot of important decisions. We wanted these rations in 1,000 or 2,000 pound increments, so we could give the readings on the mill sheets to the feed mill operator, who was mixing the feed—both on the weigh wagons and at the feed mill. The feed mill operator had our charts that were run off from our computer out in the truck with him. This was a revolutionary breakthrough in the feed industry—no one had ever effectively provided this service before.

Besides that, the feed operator was generally dealing with other problems at the same time. Oftentimes, he'd

---

*— Cal (Calorie). A unit of heat required to raise the temperature of 1 gram of water from 14.5 to 15.5 degrees centigrade.

be trying to fix his mill—because it kept breaking down. Our feedlot specialists noticed those problems and asked Cargill's management if we could send out representatives from our Plant Operations Department to make helpful suggestions about the repairing and maintaining of the feed operator's mill.

A common scenario we encountered was this: When our feedlot specialist would go out in the field to consult with the feedlot operator, he would often discover that the operator was having trouble producing the rations according to our specifications. This was often because the feed mill was broken down. Our feedlot specialist would suggest to the feedlot operator, "Let's take a look at your mill maintenance program." The operator would often reply, "I don't have a mill maintenance program." Our feedlot specialist then would say, "Well, you should have a scheduled mill maintenance program. You have to know when and how to service the mill properly—for instance, when and how to provide lubrication and other maintenance and repairs."

If the situation warranted it, the feedlot specialist might offer to send out one of Cargill's representatives from the Plant Operations Department to help correct the problem and set up an effective mill maintenance program. That was another advantage that we had that our competitors did not. We were giving the customer information that

Cargill had learned from experience over many years. We were sharing the skills and expertise that the feedlot operator needed to maintain his mill properly and become a more efficient and dependable producer. Cargill, in return, learned a great deal about the feedlot operators' mill problems.

This was particularly helpful to us in getting our foot in the door and earning respect from the large feedlot operators. Three members of Cargill's Production Department who were particularly helpful in this regard were Charlie Anderson, Ron Musech, and Terry Olson.

Cargill's production managers at the Feed Division soon picked up on this trend, and they started asking, "Now wait a minute. What's going on here? You mean we got this feedlot operator's business because we sent someone out there to help him solve problems with his mill?!" All of a sudden, Cargill considered applying this approach to some other ventures.

Maybe we've got a feedlot manager way out in the boonies and he's trying to start up something or other. Maybe some of Cargill's business expertise can help start up his business. It was a whole different sales paradigm. We weren't just out there singing "Feed Your Chicks Nutrena," jingles and broadcasting marketing information on the radio anymore. We were actually showing our customers how to problem solve and how to produce more efficiently.

Cargill Feedlot Group

In the mid to late 1960s, as I was helping to establish the Cargill Feedlot System, I started utilizing a network of respected experts within Cargill's salesforce, who would go out and talk with the large cattle feeders and establish a trusted bond with them. Five of these men in particular stood out: Dr. Al Wesley, whom everyone called "Doc" and was a highly regarded large animal veterinarian; Jerry Bergeson, one of the leading cattle feed territory managers; Bill Saba, a feedlot specialist; Wally Koers,* a newly graduated Ph.D. in beef nutrition out of the University of Nebraska; and Mark McDougall, a leading beef territory manager in Iowa.

Each year, at the end of summer/early fall, this team of experts and I would get together and select the most pressing issues from a list of current cattle feed problems for the upcoming season. This was how we became known as the Cargill Feedlot Group.

At that time, our sales territory included: Minnesota, Wisconsin, Iowa, North Dakota, South Dakota, Nebraska, Kansas, Oklahoma, and Texas. My team and I would start out by conducting background research, asking the more successful cattle feeders about problems they were facing

---

*— Cargill helped train Wally Koers as a feedlot consultant. After a couple of years, Wally branched off into business on his own and went on to become one of the most successful feedlot consultants in the industry during the 1970s, and in one particular year, was the highest ranked.

going into the coming feeding period, such as modifying the feedlot surfaces to counter the effects of El Niño or implementing the best starting methods for feeding calves or yearlings.

After we identified the problems, we started making some adjustments in the makeup of our salesforce so that we could offer practical solutions to the problems that concerned cattle feeders the most. For example, some of more successful cattle feed salesmen, headed up by territory manager Mark McDougall, started using the "walkie-talkie" system in the field, which involved "walking the cattle," with the feeder and examining the cattle droppings in an attempt to identify existing feeding problems and then correcting them.

Cargill Feedlot Seminar

Beginning in the late 1960s and continuing into the early 1980s, each late summer/early fall, we started to market the concept of a "networking family" by hosting one large annual cattle feeder meeting, which came to be known as the Cargill Feedlot Seminar. These seminars would be held in centrally located cities as Salina, Kansas; Kearney, Nebraska; and Grand Island, Nebraska. They would typically feature renowned experts and leading authorities speaking on the specifically identified problems that were anticipated in feeding cattle for the upcoming season. Various pharmaceutical companies were attracted to the large gathering of prospects and offered to help sponsor and fund sought-after speakers at our seminars. We started inviting journalists as our guests from the preeminent agricultural publications of the time, such as *The Farm Journal, Successful Farmer, Feedstuffs, Calf News,* and *Beef Magazine.* News also quickly spread among the farmer feeders, as well as the media through word of mouth. This approach ended up being very successful publicity for Cargill and did not go unnoticed by other divisions in Cargill.

Tenth Annual Nutrena Feedlot Seminar in Kearny, Nebraska, mid 1980s. Courtesy of Cargill, Incorporated.

Me (far left) welcoming feedlot operators and news people to the Tenth Annual Cargill Feedlot Seminar. Courtesy of Cargill, Incorporated.

As far as participants in the Cargill Feedlot Seminars, we would invite the more well respected and successful feedlot managers and their wives. They would usually arrive in the afternoon, check into the hotel, and pick up the program literature. That evening, we would offer a program for the entire group of feedlot operators and their

Chapter Three: My Career with Cargill

Riding the mechanical bull at the Cargill Feedlot Seminar in 1981. Courtesy of Cargill, Incorporated.

Speaking as Cargill's Director of Cattle Feed Programs in 1984 at a Feedlot Seminar in Grand Island, Nebraska. Courtesy of Cargill, Incorporated.

wives, typically featuring a motivational speaker, sports commentator, media spokesman, or humorist. Examples were Terry Bradshaw, Charlie Boon, and Tom Osborne. The next morning, we would host a breakfast for everyone, and then the ladies would go on outings, such as to a dinner theater, while the feedlot managers would attend a presentation on topics including starting cattle, the state of the market, new feeding products or new vaccines.

During this time, our Cargill Feedlot Seminars were meeting with great success, and Cargill's reputation was spreading with all of the positive publicity we were getting at these seminars, as well as through articles in the agricultural magazines, and by general word of mouth.

Part of this success was also due to the growing popularity of Cargill-Nutrena's Beef Product Management Tools,

Nutrena's Personalized Management Tool for 1987-88, and Nutrena's Cow/Calf Calendar Page 1. Courtesy of Cargill, Incorporated.

Getting It Right

which Spun Off of the Prescription Feeding Program. These included the Cow/Calf Program and the Live Calf Calendar. These programs were designed to identify what tasks must

SUPPLIES

- Veterinarian's phone number
- Drying cloth to dry calf
- Iodine spray for navel
- Injectable vitamin A
- Ear tags
- Record book
- Gloves and calf puller
- Heat lamps
- Calf scour treatments
- Syringe and needles
- Disinfectant
- Ralgro¹ gun
- Ralgro¹ implants
- Liquamycin LA-200² injectable oxyt(
- Castrating and dehorning equipmer
- Mineral feeders
- NUTRENA® beef feed supplement:

FEEDING SUGGESTIONS

- Be sure there is ample forage available. Feed extra hay if pasture is sparse.

NUTRENA products for cows	Forage Type				
	Immature	Mature	Dormant	Silage	
Beefcake® 25-12.5 block					
20% cube	2-3 lbs	2-3 lbs + 2-3 lbs grain	2 lbs		
32% cube	2-4 lbs 2-3 lbs	6-7 lbs 3-5 lbs + 1-2 lbs grain	3 lbs 2 lbs		
CR 32 liquid	2-3 lbs	2-3 lbs + 2-3 lbs grain	2 lbs		
12:12 Mineral Mag-14 mineral	Free-choice	Free-choice	Free-choice During grass tetany season	Free-choice	

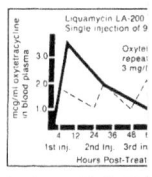

Note the sustained blood levels for long-acting Liquamycin LA-200, a treatments of a conventional oxyt

This level for treatment of 1) caused by Pasteurella spp. (shipp Bovine Keratoconjunctivitis (p Moraxell bovis.

- Increase grain or cubes 2 to 4 lbs each day for cows in poor condition.
- Inject Liquamycin' LA-200, if necessary. Liquamycin' LA-200 creates a depot effect at the injection site. From here, clinically effective medication levels are gradually metered out for 72 hours — that's 3 full days. So your animals get rest instead of retreatment stress.

MANAGEMENT SUGGESTIONS

⊙ Predetermine date calves due to start arriving.
   Most calf losses occur either at or within 36 hours after birth. Most are the result of calving problems. Watch cow closely during calving and render assistance. Check cows twice daily.

- Calving difficulties ahead if:
  - only the calf's tail is visible.
  - only the calf's head is visible.
  - front feet protrude past the knees, but the calf's nose cannot be located.
  - the head and one foot are visible.
  - more than two feet are visible.
  - after two hours of labor there is no progress in delivery. **Secure help!**
  - pulling calf, use sash cord and **down**, not straight out.
  - "calf puller" is used, be sure the presentation of the calf is normal.

⊙ Please mark these dates on your management calendar

¹Ralgro® is a registered trademark of International Minerals & Chemical Corp.
²Liquamycin® LA-200 is a trademark of Pfizer, Inc.

- Watch for scours.
  A newborn calf will receive its greatest amount protection from the antibodies found in the colostru of the dam. The first 4 to 6 hours are the most critic: and a calf should nurse at least twice during th time. Consult a veterinarian about use of antibo(products and scours treatment programs.

- Give an injection of vitamins A and D, a few days aft birth to insure adequate vitamin levels.
- Spray the navel cord with iodine spray as soon a possible after birth.
- Separate pregnant cows from cows with calves.
⊙ Record birth date.
- Identify calf with ear tags and/or tatoos.
- Dehorn and castrate calves during first month of ag
- Implant calves with Ralgro¹ (except those to b(used as replacements.)

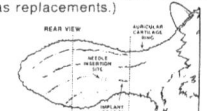

Nutrena's Cow/Calf Calendar Page 2. Courtesy of Cargill, Incorporated.

Chapter Three: My Career with Cargill

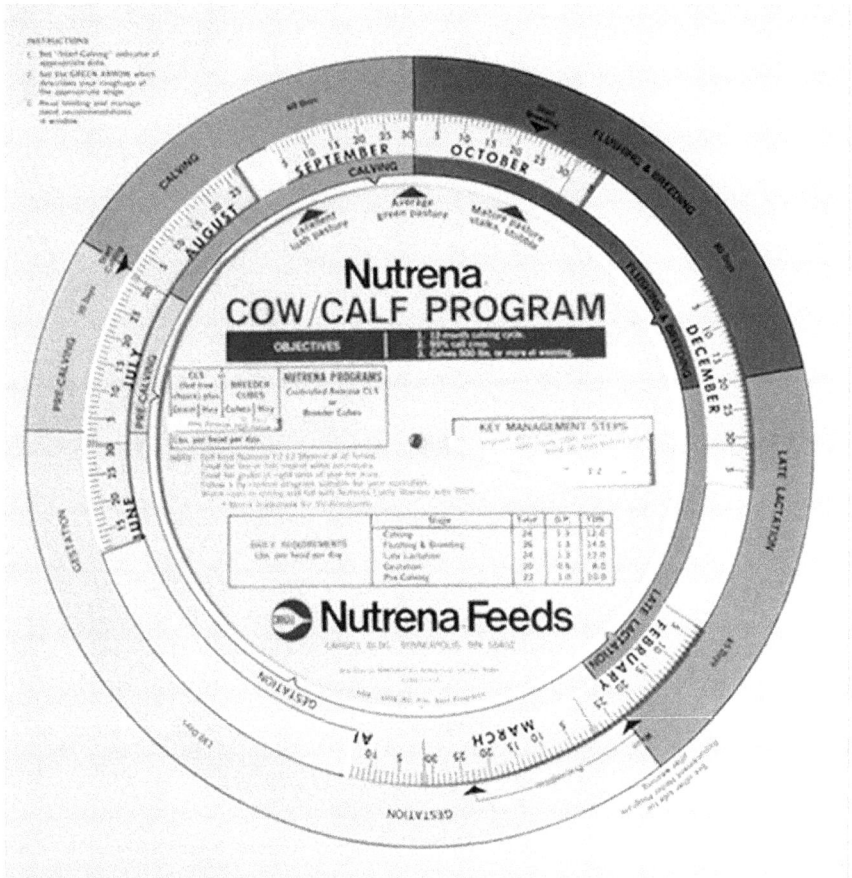

Nutrena's Cow/Calf Program wheel chart describing the stages of a cow's gestation period. Courtesy of Cargill, Incorporated.

be timed correctly in breeding and raising calves and to outline what tasks are to be carried out, when, who is responsible for that task, why it is necessary and in many cases, how to complete it. This management tool was also applied to pigs with the Three Stage Sow Program. The basic concepts were the same.

Aerial view of the Caprock Operation at Leoti, Kansas, in the mid-1970s. Each pen contains 250 cattle. Courtesy of Cargill, Incorporated.

Caprock Industries

From February 1975 to the time of my retirement in 1988, I was responsible for calculating the rations for the Caprock Feedlots.

As part of the Caprock initiative, Cargill had purchased some of the larger feedlots in the United States, including two in Gruver, Texas, and shortly afterward a larger feedlot in Dalhart, Texas and then one further north in Leoti, Kansas. Over the years, Caprock, which was headquartered in Gruver, Texas, grew from 64,000 head capacity to 265,000 head capacity and fed over 3,500,000 cattle per year. At the peak of my career with Cargill, I was responsible for a considerable number of these cattle. In fact, according to the Consulting Nutritionist Top Ten List, dated March 6, 1985, I was ranked as the 8th leading feedlot consultant in the U.S. in terms of number of cattle being managed at that time, with over 203,000 under my supervision.

Annual Cargill Marketing Meeting

The Annual Cargill Marketing Meeting was a master meeting for the product managers in the Feed Division to develop plans to market new products for the coming year.

During the late 1970s to 1980s, Bruce Priebe, Feed Division Marketing Director, introduced an overall strategy that promoted annual marketing plans to introduce new products and programs and enhance or replace existing programs. Cargill's Product Managers gathered in meetings in different cities, such as Duluth, Tampa, San Diego, New Prague, etc. to present their marketing plans for the year ahead. Each marketing plan would first be approved by the marketing director, and then the product managers would explain their marketing plan to the other product managers at the Annual Cargill Marketing Meeting. These marketing meetings were held each year at the beginning of the crop year, around June 1st, from around 1980 through 1988. I felt that these meetings

One of Nutrena's marketing campaigns featuring a Wild West theme. I played the part of "sheriff" (front row, far left). Courtesy of Cargill, Incorporated.

Posing as sheriff for the Wild West Marketing Campaign. Courtesy of Cargill, Incorporated.

helped present more ambitious sales challenges to master, as well as promoting some healthy competition and creativity.

Key Marketing Colleagues

There were two particularly outstanding individuals who were instrumental in helping Nutrena's Feed Division successfully move products during my tenure there: Fred Saltvold, Advertising Manager, Feed, and Bert Gibbs, Government Regulation Manager, Feed. Fred Saltvold was extremely gifted at capturing our marketing concepts on paper and designing marketing brochures and other

Von and I with Fred and Elaine Saltvold and others at a Northern Regional Personnel Meeting; Fred and Von in center; Elaine and I at far right. Courtesy of Cargill, Incorporated.

marketing materials. Bert Gibbs helped tremendously in navigating the legal intricacies of Nutrena's marketing practices and in helping us obtain needed clearances through the Food and Drug Administration. He was especially helpful when it came to clearances with antibiotics and feed additive combinations.

Both Fred and Bert were truly talented individuals who were able to interpret and explain complex concepts clearly. Both were a big part of Cargill's marketing success in the Feed Division.

PART TWO: MY INVOLVEMENT WITH CARGILL'S RESEARCH AND MARKETING INNOVATIONS

The Challenge to Increase Technological Advances in the Feed Industry

In 1955, when I first started with the company, Cargill had an experimental farm in Pleasant Hill, Missouri. I think they had a handful of sows and laying hens—that was it. Jim Hamilton, Product Development and Improvement Manager, was running the farm, and he was feeding different types of rations to hens. Jim wondered what would happen if he fed fat to the hens, so he decided to give it a try. Low and behold, he discovered that he got more eggs on less pounds of ration. Of course, that was because by adding fat, he was feeding higher energy feed. This was the type of research that was being done at that time—basic trial and error. Jim made the observation that he got more eggs per pound of ration when he fed fat, so Cargill came up with a new feed. That was one way Cargill's personnel tried to increase their business. They would come up with something new to talk about and would then *keep* trying to come up with something new in a timely fashion. A few of the large feed companies used this strategy to some extent. Our largest competitor, Purina, was good at that. They seemed to have had a different angle every year. It might not perform as well as last year, but at least it was new and different. It had been a while since Cargill's Feed Division had come out with anything new, and the personnel in the office got to thinking about this.

I didn't really have anything to do with that particular poultry feed project. I just stood on the sidelines and watched it. They called Hamilton's new egg feed, "Fifty Grand." Some of our feed mills got into trouble right off the bat in implementing this program, because they were trying to process fat in their feed without the right kind of metal, which resulted in rancid feed. In addition, when the feed was stored in paper sacks, the fat tended to bleed through the bag. It's similar to how a popcorn sack gets too much butter and gets grease spots on it.

During this time of trial and error with our feed experiments in the 1950s, it was just one thing after another; two steps forward and one step back. I will never forget one particular incident; I was there when it happened. Ralph Grier, the Feed Division Director at that time, suggested that our salesforce offer a guarantee whereby anyone who fed our fat-enhanced feed would get 20% more eggs per hen. I guess Ralph didn't know exactly what he meant by a guarantee, but I distinctly remember what happened afterwards. The sales pitch worked. Cargill sold more egg feed and had larger flocks on the Fifty Grand Program, but there were some definite drawbacks to this fat-enhanced feed. For one thing, it caused the chickens to crave more fiber. If you put more energy in the ration without the added fiber, the chickens would go looking for the additional fiber they needed to digest that energy. The sales department at the Central Office started getting claims regarding problems with the feed. When there was a serious claim, and the territory manager couldn't handle it adequately, the sales department would send out a district sales manager to resolve it.

I was at a sales meeting in Minneapolis, and there was a sales manager there named Ole Sonstegard. Ole went out to talk to a farmer feeder about his claim. I was attending a sales meeting when Ole came back. He said, "You've never seen anything like it! I went into this chicken house, and there were a bunch of hens that didn't have any feathers." Then he said, "And you won't believe this, but those chickens started pecking at my shoes. I thought they were going to peck my shoelaces off!" Ole's eyes were as big as saucers! I will never forget that as long as I live.

I thought to myself, "Gosh—Central Office is sure paying off a lot of claims." But you know why that was? Evidently, they hadn't run tests first with laying hens to find out where the bugs were.

Back when I was teaching Vo Ag in northwestern Iowa, a certain feed company belonging to one of Cargill's competitors came out to hold a meeting in Storm Lake, and I was aware that they had fat in their feed. Sure enough, the fat would bleed through those sacks. When this happened, the customers would call up the feed company and tell them to come and take back the feed that had been sold to them. The feed company didn't like that, of course. I suspected the sacks were going to bleed before it even happened.

In the late 1950s, much of the time with most feed manufacturers, including Cargill to a large extent, the industry operated basically through trial and error. The feed companies knew they needed to keep coming up with something new, but the new products weren't necessarily tested out completely. These companies were torn between pressures to present new marketing angles and new sales pitches and the need to thoroughly test new products.

This trial and error approach helped us in the long run, because it taught the salesforce at Cargill a valuable lesson, and fortunately we never forgot it. If the new product involved an outside company, we learned that it was critically important to take the company's recommendations and implement them as instructed with multiple animals under controlled conditions to see what happened before the Cargill salesforce started selling the product all around the country.

Cargill Nutrena's Research Farm

In the late 1950s, Dick Baldwin was hired as Research Director, to centralize research at Cargill, and the Nutrena Research Farm was established in Elk River, Minnesota. This research farm helped us to enter a new era of utilizing field-tested and proven technology as applied to the science of animal feed.

One example of how we learned about the importance of field-testing products before marketing them on a broad-scale was when Rumensin was first introduced to the cattle feeder in the mid-1970s.

Rumensin is a cost-effective feed additive that improves feed efficiency by providing more energy from the ration. Even from the time the product was first launched,

Aerial view of Nutrena Research Farm in Elk River, Minnesota, circa 1960s. Courtesy of Cargill, Incorporated.

Rumensin was considered to be the greatest thing since sliced bread; however, our Cattle Feed Division at Cargill decided to check out the product at the research farm before we marketed it. We found out very quickly that you can throw cattle off their feed regimen if you administer the Rumensin additive at full strength all at once, as was originally instructed by the additive producer. Rumensin changes the energy balance in the ration, which in turn can change the balance of bacteria in the cow's stomach, and then the animal can potentially produce too much acid too fast. If that happens, then the animal can quit eating and potentially develop acidosis. We sent our territory managers out and instructed the farmer feeder how to introduce Rumensin in the right way—how to work up to it gradually, but other farmer feeders who were on other company's programs were introducing it way too quickly and not gradually increasing the amounts fed to the cattle. This turned out to be a real problem for them.

Another example of what can go wrong with failing to field test new products happened in the 1970s. In about 1978, representatives of our Cargill salesforce traveled to Kansas, and we found out that there was an epidemic of some kind going on in the large cattle feed yards. We started putting two and two together and found that all of the sick cattle were eating feed that was being sold by one of our larger competitors. This company, we heard, was using a new and different oil meal. It was a castor bean meal, and it tended to upset the calves' digestive system. This discovery helped us, because all of a sudden we realized what the problem was, and we felt that we could help the feeders out by calling on a particular company's customers and asking, "You've got sick cattle, right?" We didn't advertise the fact that we knew it, but we were aware that the feeder probably had cattle with digestive problems. We mentioned other feeders in the area that were in the same boat, and we knew those cattle feeders were all using "Brand X" Feed. Before long, our salesforce was successful in gaining the trust of those particular cattle feeders, and they were anxious to hear about what we had to say. Over time, these experiences resulted in a major push for our salesforce to get our own research right.

Three-Stage Sow Feeding Program

Cargill's Feed Division accomplished some great innovations at our research farm. One of the most important breakthroughs that happened there involved swine, in the mid to late 1950s, when Francis Wingert, Cargill's Ph.D. Swine Nutritionist, and I, as Acting Swine Products Manager, developed the 3-Stage Sow Feeding Program. Francis and I worked very well as a team.

Chapter Three: My Career with Cargill

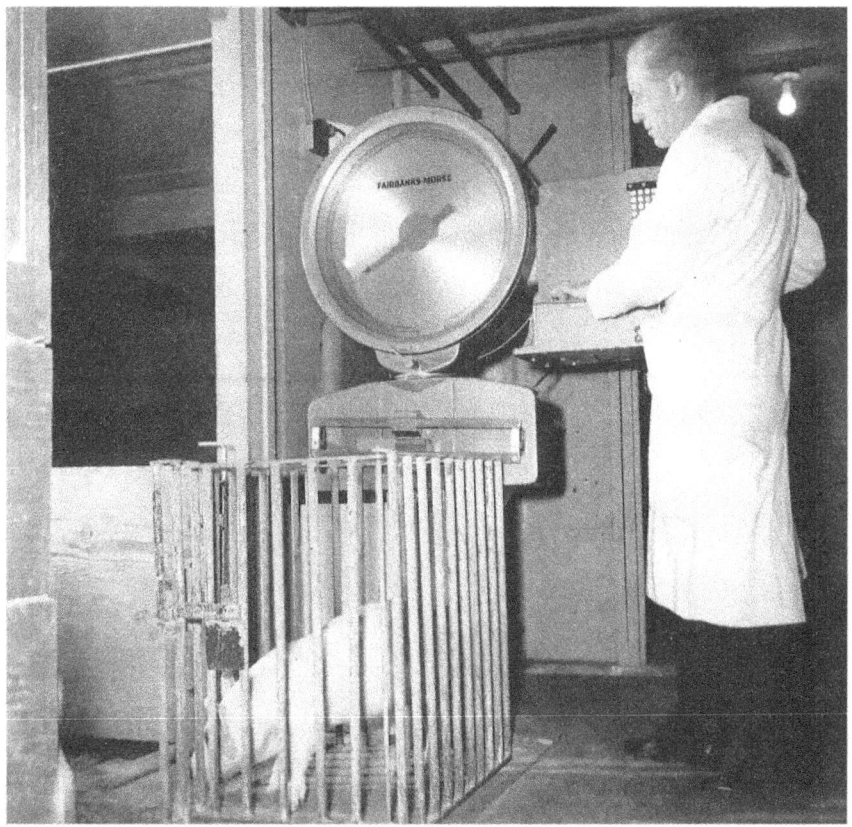

Francis Wingert, Swine Research Manager, at Nutrena's Research Farm. Courtesy of Cargill, Incorporated.

Nutrena's 3-Stage Sow Feeding Program was instrumental in revolutionizing Cargill's hog business for a long period of time into the future, and it eventually spread throughout the entire industry. We figured out that the biggest nutritional problems in hog production were related to gestating and lactating sows. Many hog feeders were allowing their gestating sows to self-feed, i.e.,

Getting It Right

eat as much as they wanted whenever they wanted, and these sows and gilts were getting too fat. This fat tended to develop around the reproductive organs, and it had a detrimental effect, because it would reduce the blood supply to the embryos, resulting in a small litter of underweight

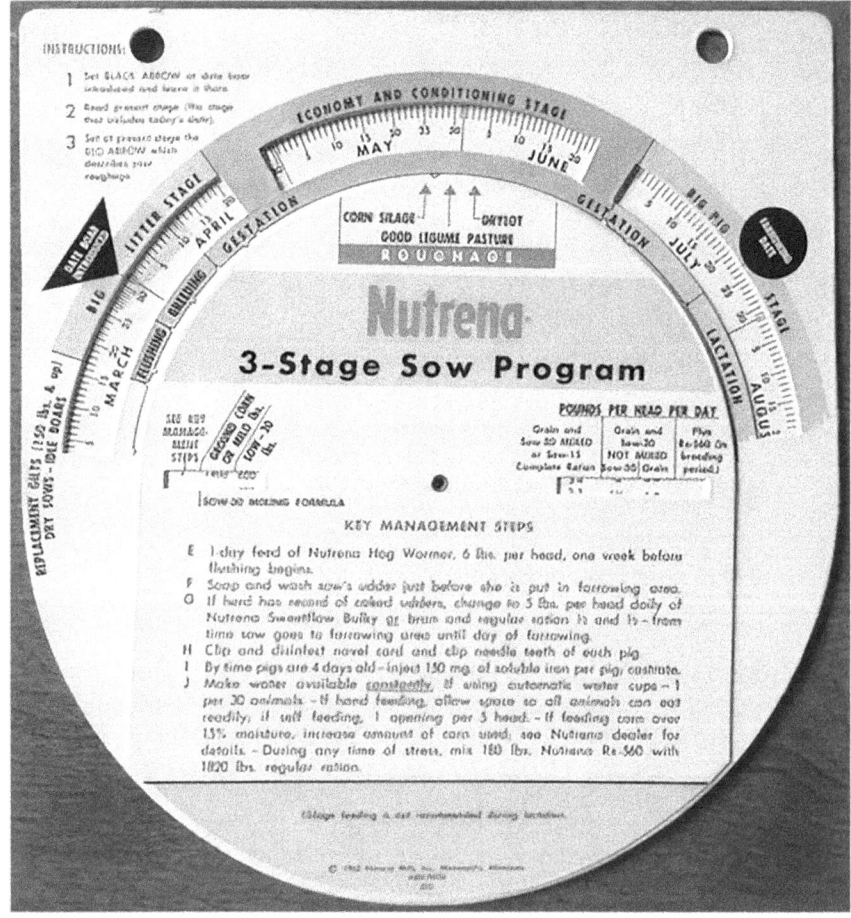

Nutrena's 3-Stage Sow Program wheel chart. Courtesy of Cargill, Incorporated.

pigs. Through our research, Francis and I found out that if you carefully fed the sows ample energy in balanced rations at a high level at the time they were being bred, it greatly increased the likelihood that they would produce more eggs, resulting in more embryos to fertilize. We discovered that if we then cut that feed way back at the critical time of the gestation period (for about 60 days), then we would prevent the sow from getting too fat. In addition, we economized by saving feed.

Working on a 3-Stage Sow Program Presentation with Charlie Boon, Radio Broadcasting Legend. Courtesy of Cargill, Incorporated.

It is natural for the sow to be hungry during that critical 60-day gestational period when you are limiting her to four pounds of feed a day. Sows will overeat if allowed to do so, but if you limit them to only four pounds of balanced ration once a day, during the identified stages of the gestational period, then they don't have the opportunity to consume the unnecessary energy that causes them to develop excess fat. We found out that if we increase the feed intake quite drastically about three weeks before the sows are about to farrow, this will stimulate the mammary glands, leading to increased milk production, which will result in stronger, healthier piglets. If the sows are in good shape, they will do a better job feeding their big litters of baby pigs, and, what a difference! A lot depends on the timing and amounts of the feed levels of a balanced ration.

Development of the Isolation Systems

PIGLOOS

The "Pigloo" was the brain child of Jim Collins, who was an Isolation and Antibody Specialist from Waukon, Iowa. The Pigloo was the forerunner of the Isolet, which was an integral part of the isolation system for swine production. Jim Collins and his team had been researching and developing the idea of an isolation system for raising pigs for quite a while, and Clarence Whitworth, Feed Division Marketing Director, learned about this concept after meeting Jim at a National Swine Association meeting in the early 1960s. Clarence became intrigued with using the concept of "the Pigloo," and Cargill's Swine Research Team (which included Clarence Whitworth, Jim Collins, Francis Wingert and myself), spent considerable time in the 1960s exploring how we could capitalize on this idea in the Feed Division at Cargill. The isolation system fit into an innovative approach that was going on at that time in our part of the feed industry; that was, helping the producer—letting him know that Cargill was a company with a wide range of resource assistance to offer. Jim Collins and the rest of our Swine Research Team envisioned that the isolation system could provide that kind of help.

This isolation system served the purpose of keeping baby pigs healthy. Baby pigs, like most animals, tend to get sick easily when they are very young and vulnerable. They aren't born with the resistance against many organisms that they're exposed to after birth. When you keep a group of sows together, and they're farrowing in a central location, then you get a mixture and transfer of disease organisms. Once that transfer starts, if it is a certain kind of bug, the baby pig can get digestive upsets potentially resulting in scours diarrhea, which can prove to be fatal. Instead of getting a nice big litter of nine or ten piglets, the farmer is going to wind up with significantly smaller and less healthy litters that are going to take much longer to get to market.

When the complete isolation system was used, it was proven to be effective by Cargill's own research team. The concept was to give the sow her own little compartment. When you put the sow in the Isolet before the piglets are born, she was exposed to any organism that was in there, and she developed antibodies against any disease organisms that were in the colostrum milk that she produced. After the baby pigs were born, they gained disease protection from that milk, and they weren't getting exposed to other pigs and their diseases. A specified number of days after birth when the piglets were capable of producing their own antibodies, our Cargill consultants recommended that the farmer wean the baby pigs from the sow, and we built these individual units consisting of hutches with feeding floors out in front.

Cargill's isolation system for swine proved to be economical. It was the most practical, low cost unit that has ever been developed to house hogs. There are so many reasons why it works. The pigs go into the hutches, they bed down, and the low roof helps hold the heat down on them in cold weather. The isolation system helps them maintain their body heat so they're more comfortable. The pigs won't mess in the unit, because they don't mess in their nest. Instead, they go out in the yard and mess. Another advantage is that the back of the hutch opens up, enabling a breeze to blow through in the warmer weather, and helping to keep the hogs cool and contented. The swine isolation system typically costs far less than what a big centralized facility would cost.

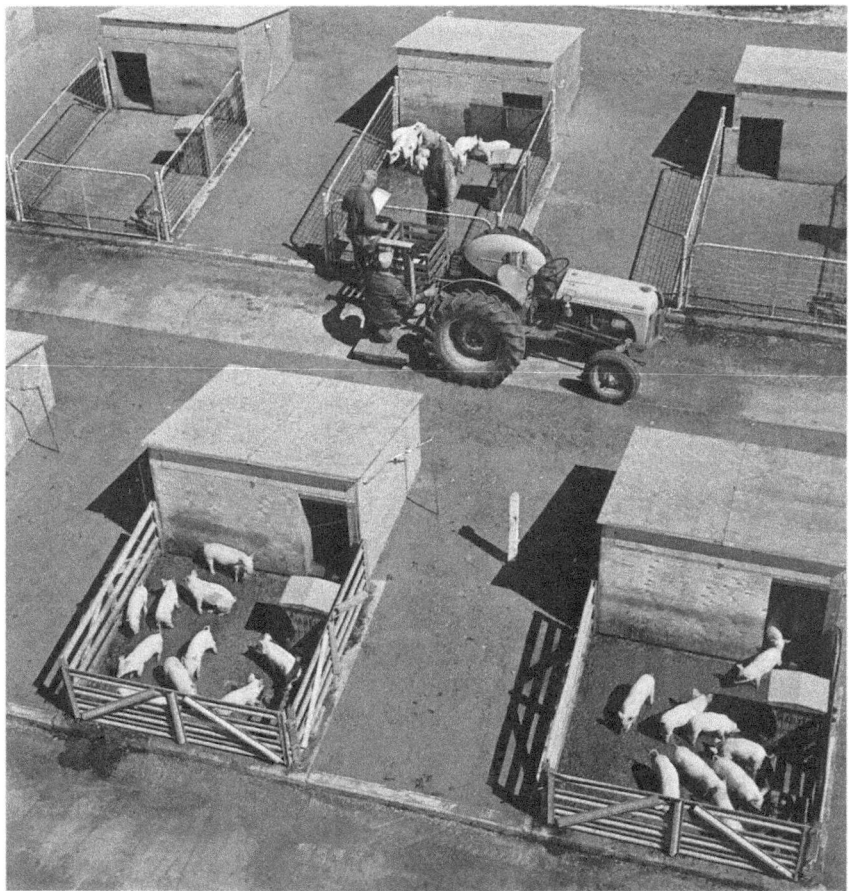

Pig Isolation System at the Nutrena Research Farm. Courtesy of Cargill, Incorporated.

Because Cargill advocated for the farmers to build this swine isolation system, our Feed Division had detailed plans drawn up so that the producers could build their own Isolets. This isolation system required a lot of the Cargill salesman. He had to invest a considerable amount of time in the farmer's process of building and establishing the isolation units, and that took time away from the salesman selling other products and helping to keep the feed mills running. Also, the isolation system turned out to be high maintenance and labor intensive for the farmer, who in wintertime, understandably tended to think more of his own comfort than he did of his pigs'. Particularly in the northern climates, the farmer didn't like going out and taking care of those pigs in the cold weather. He sometimes had to use a snowplow to get to each one of the Isolets and then haul the feed over to them. Consequently, the isolation system morphed into a system of hutches and feeding floors, which are still quite prevalent in farms throughout the Midwest to this day.

CALFLOOS

During the 1960s, the problem that the pig farmers were having paled in comparison to the problems dairy farmers were having with their calves. In the Feed Division at Cargill, we noticed that a large share of dairy calves—about 25% of them—never reached maturity, because they

Chapter Three: My Career with Cargill

contracted contagious diseases, such as pneumonia and diarrhea. Some died and others got sick and recovered but still did not resume a normal growth rate. It was a tremendous financial loss, because the farmers were putting all these calves together, and they often would even feed them out of the same bucket. As a result, the calves couldn't help but get exposed to each other's diseases. The mother cows couldn't develop all of the necessary antibodies to protect their calves, because the calves were all housed together.

Me with one of Nutrena's first Calfloos at the Nutrena Research Farm in 1958. Courtesy of Cargill, Incorporated.

Providing calves with the first milk from their mothers, which is called the colostrum milk, gives them many of the antibodies to the diseases that they will be exposed to.

Rows of calf isolation units at the Research Farm. Courtesy of Cargill, Incorporated.

This helps the calf gain strength. The calves like the colostrum and drink it readily. Then the farmer puts the calf in the isolation unit, which helps him avoid exposure to any other calves. The farmer can put a heat lamp in the unit when the weather is really cold. The engineers in our Feed Division designed a plywood house that was made out of certain standard measurements and provided plans to the dairyman helping him produce the house at a lower cost, minimizing waste in lumber and labor. The dairymen could then build these Calfloos economically by themselves.

Companies such as Impro Products, Inc. out of Waukon, Iowa, have since taken over the manufacturing of the isolation units for calves, which are now constructed out of plastic or fiberglass. Calfloos can be seen sitting out in the larger dairy farms, sometimes hundreds in a group, in states such as Wisconsin. You don't see very many dairy farms without them. The Calfloo did even more to reduce the mortality and disease rate in the dairy industry than the isolation system in the swine industry, because the calf is isolated before it was exposed to too many harmful organisms. The Cargill Feed Division would recommend that the calf is then fed a "milk replacer" designed for optimum nutrition for the growing animal. The milk replacer was artificial milk with antibiotics in it, providing additional protection from diseases.

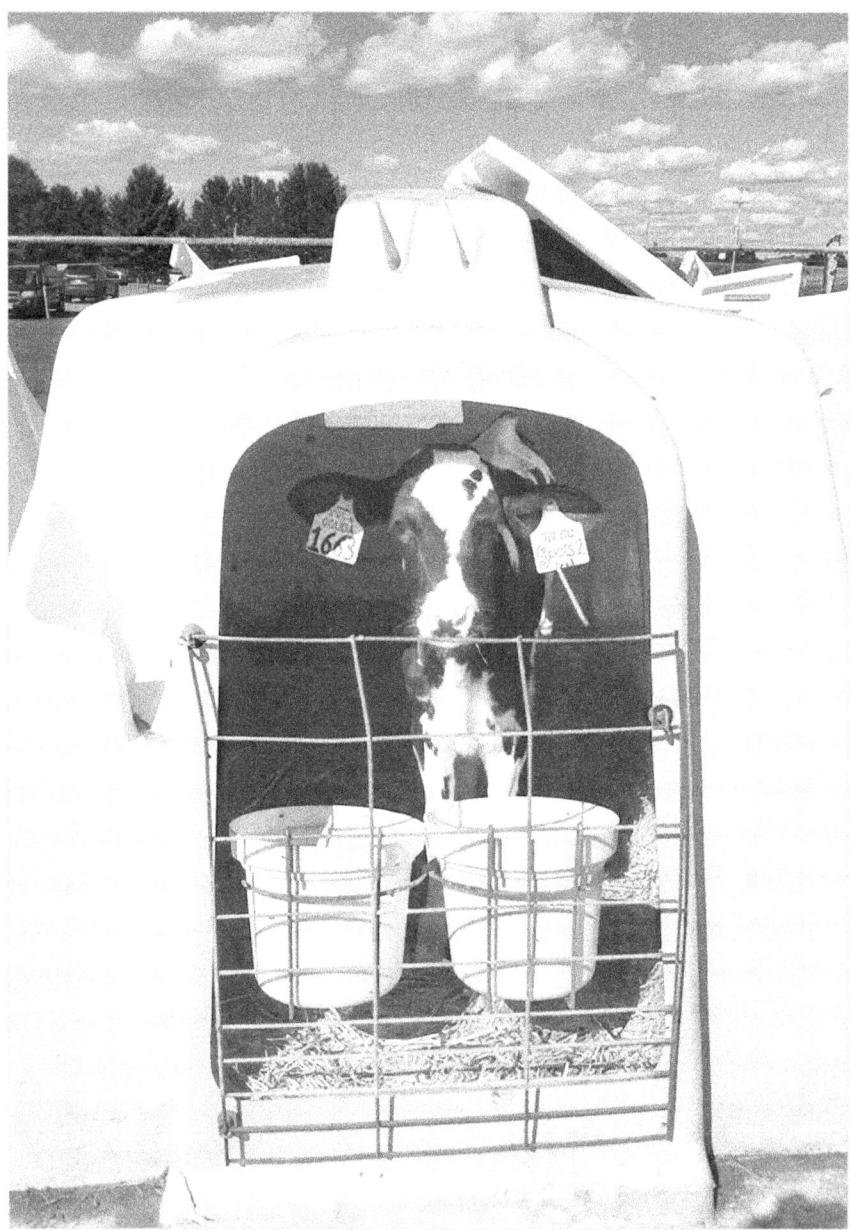

Modern day calf isolation unit at Marieke's Dairy Farm in Thorp, Wisconsin, 2020.

Chapter Three: My Career with Cargill

A large number of calf isolation units on a dairy farm near Rock Falls, Wisconsin, 2016.

The Role of Pharmaceuticals

The role of pharmaceuticals in Cargill's Feed Division was very important. Many new antibiotics and combinations of antibiotics were being introduced in the 1950s, and this was a real game changer in the animal feed industry. Cargill's Feed Division had an evolving, overlapping disease protection program. We wanted to prevent the animal from developing a resistance to any one antibiotic, so we changed the way we administered the antibiotics used in the recommended feeding programs. We had used this approach primarily in our hog program. Pigs have a simpler digestive system than cattle, and it is more similar to humans. In Cargill's swine feed program, pigs were fed different feeds as they grew to be different sizes. For instance, the younger piglets were fed Creep-20, which was 20% protein, and then as they got bigger and started eating more feed, they switched to Pre Shoat 16 Feed, which was 16% protein. As we reduced the protein levels of the feed, we would correspondingly change the type and level of antibiotic. We did this in order to prevent resistance to any one type of antibiotic and to prevent any one drug from building up in the animal's tissues.

Cargill's Feed Division was responsive to the medical community's concerns about misuse of antibiotics, and we tried to be sensitive to the public's perceptions as well. We also made it a point to get along as well as we could with the pharmaceutical representatives. We wanted to make sure Cargill was carefully following all the rules and regulations involved with the drug clearances through the Food and Drug Administration.

Naturally, the pharmaceutical companies wanted to work with Cargill, because we had a large share of the animal feed business as well as solid relationships with many of the producers who used the products these companies sold. We worked hard together to foster these mutually beneficial business relationships.

Chapter Three: My Career with Cargill

During the late 1950s through the early 1980s, the Cargill Feed Division would sponsor what we referred to as "Day-Long" Feeder Meetings/Super Feeder Meetings every fall throughout the Midwest. At these meetings, I would present information about Cargill's research on the latest feed supplements and other supporting products, such as wormers and vaccinations. The pharmaceutical companies would often help line up a speaker and help pay the speaking fee. Sometimes the speaker would be a celebrity and sometimes an expert in the field, and sometimes it

Nutrena Territory Managers at a Cargill Feeder Meeting in the 1980s with Terry Bradshaw (back row in white cowboy hat). Courtesy of Cargill, Incorporated.

was a combination of the two. Cargill's territory managers would typically team up with a pharmaceutical rep in different booths to explain our various products to the cattle feeders. We would assign a pharmaceutical rep and a territory manager to each and would hold contests. We would run a competition with these pharmaceutical reps, and our sales people would vote on the winner, deciding who was doing the best job of helping Cargill to represent the products. At the end of the day, our salesforce would award a trophy to the pharmaceutical rep who had done the best job of selling. The pharmaceutical reps thought that was really something! I'm pretty sure that the winners would go home and tell their bosses about the fact that they needed a raise because they won the trophy from Cargill's Feed Division.

Nutrena's Controlled Release Liquid Supplement

Cows love molasses, but when you combine molasses with urea protein, the cows can potentially run into urea poisoning if they consume too much. Urea is high in nitrogen, and cows need nitrogen to increase the bacteria in their stomach to break down and digest their feed. Cattle can ingest too much nitrogen if they eat too much urea protein, because protein is 16% nitrogen. Nitrogen content is related to bacteria. The higher the nitrogen content, the more bacteria—and gas—you have. Cattle need a certain amount of bacteria to digest their food, but they can get too much and then they get urea poisoning. Liquid molasses tastes really good to cattle, so they want to eat a lot of it. It helps the feed to be palatable, but you don't want cattle to ingest too much protein and thus too much nitrogen and then get urea molasses poisoning.

Cargill didn't recommend feeding our cattle liquid molasses prior to the 1960s, and our Feed Division didn't sell liquid supplement with urea in it because of concerns about toxicity. Our specialists didn't encourage the cattle feeders to use it, and the feeders generally avoided it. We recommended that the farmers "feed what we sold," which up to that point was the dry pelleted complete protein supplement with vitamins and minerals that we called Nutrena Beef Cake. Then in the 1960s, Cargill's laboratory research revealed that if you heat and mix urea and molasses together in the right proportions at the right time, it will bind some of the nitrogen in the urea, and consequently, you will effectively reduce the toxicity in the mixture. Back in the old days of the industry, before the mid 1950s, the cattle feeders liked to feed pure oil meal, because it didn't have urea in it.

We started selling Cargill's molasses controlled liquid supplement in our Nutrena Cattle Feed Product Line in the mid-1970s, several years after the Molasses Division

Promoting Nutrena's CLS Product at the Cargill display booth in the exhibit area of a trade show. Courtesy of Cargill, Incorporated.

of Cargill discovered a way to bind the nitrogen and reduce the absorption and therefore the toxicity to the animal. It was called Nutrena's Controlled-Release Liquid Supplement (CLS), and it was a patented process.

Prior to that time, Cargill's Molasses Division was actually competing with the Feed Division of Cargill. Our Feed Division's CLS sales took off immediately-the cattle loved it! Also, our salesforce devised a very successful marketing plan to promote the product. We noticed that many

Nutrena's Controlled Release Liquid Supplement, CLS. Courtesy of Cargill, Incorporated.

small rural towns had movie theaters that weren't doing so well since television had been introduced. We contacted the owners of the theaters to ask if they would be receptive to us renting their facility to show a film for entertainment along with a film Cargill produced explaining the benefits of CLS. The theater owners thought this

Getting It Right

Nutrena's Controlled Release Liquid Supplement, CLS. Courtesy of Cargill, Incorporated.

was a great idea and were all for it. It was just like the old days of movie-going, with the popcorn and the whole nine yards. We first showed our 25-minute film on Nutrena's Controlled Release Liquid Supplement. Then we'd show a documentary-type film that Tink Klang, a travel consultant, had put together called "Edge of the Arctic Ice." The

Chapter Three: My Career with Cargill

Promoting Nutrena's CLS Supplement along with the film, "The Edge of the Arctic Ice." Courtesy of Cargill, Incorporated.

film was about Klang traveling up to the North Pole and stalking an enormous polar bear. Klang gets the bear in his sights and then he changes his mind and decides not to shoot it after all. It was a riveting story.

Classes for Territory Managers at the Research Farm

Starting in the 1960s and continuing throughout the 1970s, our Cargill Feed Division took a unique approach with our feedlot customers in terms of training dealers out in the field, which turned out to be highly effective. Our district territory managers were telling us that the beef feeding system was complicated and that it was difficult to know everything about it, so they would send key dealers and field salesman for training sessions at the Research Farm in Elk River.

I have many pictures of class participants grinding away in the basement of the Kemathese Motel nearby the Research Farm. We would bring in classes of 20 to 30 of Cargill's territory managers at a time, and eventually, large feed dealers, and field representatives, who were also referred to as country salesmen.

After the district territory manager got up to a certain point of expertise, he could train his own dealers. We would also have meetings in central locations such as Sioux City. We would bring the large dealers in and we would get them sold on the fact that "this is what can help *me*," but then the dealers would need to follow up and help train their own field representatives.

There were two types of classes—those consisting of the Cargill salesforce and those consisting of the salesforce

Chapter Three: My Career with Cargill

outside of Cargill. The number of classes taught per year would depend on how many Cargill salesmen we needed to train and then how many dealers wanted to send in their country salesmen based on the number of identified high

GATHERED TO LEARN are cattle feeders and territory managers at Council Bluffs, Ia., where one of many Nutrena courses — this taught health maintenance in beef herds — are held throughout the Midwest. Shown are, top row: Chuck Smith, territory manager, Sioux City; Harold Hundley, feedlot manager, Nebraska; Dave Kesteloot, Producer Marketing department, Marshall, Minn.; Mike McGuire, T.M., Sioux City; Tom Swoyer, T.M., Sioux City; Ken Dvorak, feedlot manager, Nebraska; second row: Don Awe, animal health products manager, Minneapolis; Bob Mayberry, T.M., Sioux City; Owen Kliegl, T.M., Sioux City; Paul Blankinship, T.M., Grand Island; Bob Pape, Grand Island; Wayne Nissen, T.M., Rowan, Iowa; Dr. Al Wesley, veterinarian, Kansas City; Leroy Whiting, T.M., Grand Island; Carl Meldahl, T.M., Minneapolis; and Keith Lohse, T.M., Minneapolis; third row: Don Lyons, T.M., Grand Island; Bud Thee, T.M., Rowan; Laverne Brown, T.M., Kansas City; John Riebeling, T.M., Sioux City; Chuck Nitsch, T.M., Sioux City; and Lloyd Davis, T.M., Rowan.

JIM MCDOUGALL, in charge of beef feed sales for Nutrena, is deeply involved in providing computer services to feeder-customers so the last ounce of animal weight may be had at the least expense.

One of our many Nutrena classes for territory managers and beef feeders, this one on health maintenace of beef herds, in Council Bluffs, Iowa, 1973. Courtesy of Cargill, Incorporated.

potential beef districts. The classes would wind up being about five days long, and we would put on a real show for the participants. I would often work with the classes out at Elk River for the entire week. In these classes, we wouldn't mix the independent dealer salespeople in with the Cargill salesforce. They were trained separately. We didn't want the outside participants overriding the Cargill personnel.

Mike Korfeitis, the manager of the Kemathese Hotel, was an excellent cook, and he took very good care of us in the culinary department.

We enjoyed some lighter moments during these trainings. For example, the participants would usually arrive on a bus, and when they got off, we would weigh them, "just like cattle." Then at the end of the training week, we would weigh them again before they left. We would calculate the average daily gain and loss of the participants and have prizes for the class member who gained the most. As a joke, we would have "wormer medicine" for the guys who didn't gain anything or lost weight, that kind of thing. We had a lot of fun.

Marketing and Salesmanship Aspects

An account of my career with Cargill would not be complete without underscoring the importance of salesmanship and marketing strategies. The concept of salesmanship

Chapter Three: My Career with Cargill

often gets a bad rap, but it actually requires a very complex set of skills that are incredibly valuable in the business world. There was a lot of psychology involved in dealing effectively with customers. In the marketing department at Cargill, we listened to our customers very carefully. We paid attention to a lot of details about them. We noticed

With Bob Mason, Division Manager, during one of Nutrena's marketing campaigns. Courtesy of Cargill, Incorporated.

that our customer probably had a banker that he trusted to handle his financial matters. He probably had a veterinarian that he called upon when he had health problems with his animals that he couldn't handle himself. He probably had a supplier. These, along with others, constituted his "team." One of the driving motivations of the Cargill Sales Department was to get on our customer's production team and become his feed supplier.

In order to get on our customer's team, we had to become almost like a family member to him. One of our strategies was to invite our customer, who was often a farmer feeder, to our Cargill Feedlot Seminar, which was a combination of work and social activities. In some special cases, we also invited the wives to come along. We'd line up a highly respected expert for our customers to listen to, who would speak about identified problems and concerns that the farmer feeder was currently facing that season, and maybe feature a celebrity or two to provide motivation and/or entertainment. Before long, this approach resulted in the customer relying on us more and more for help with his feeding program. The more the customer started relying on us for our help and expertise with his feeding needs, the more valuable we became to him. Customers found out that they had a lot to gain from Cargill.

We noticed that over time, was the farmer feeders would attend Cargill's feedlot seminars and would find them to be so helpful that they wouldn't want to miss it the next year. Before long, the farmer feeder wasn't going to do anything with his feed unless he talked to us at Cargill first. It's similar to when you go to your specialists—your doctor, your dentist, or your lawyer—it's an ongoing partnership. That ongoing partnership with the customer is a key factor in successful salesmanship. A lot of companies don't understand that. Fortunately, Cargill did.

Litigation

One of the situations Cargill tried very hard to avoid was getting involved in litigation; however, if there was something the company disliked even more, it was losing litigation once involved. To my knowledge, Cargill did not get involved in many lawsuits, but when this happened, Cargill fought to win.

It was a serious challenge to know the laws and rules Cargill had to abide by, and it was also a constant worry that a member of the company might inadvertently do something that would trigger legal action. Cargill was prepared to take on and prevent a high percentage of these types of situations by devising excellent training programs. Cargill also acquired a staff of outstanding corporate attorneys, including Jed Hepworth, and charged them with preventing costly litigious situations from happening

Getting It Right

H. JED HEPWORTH
ATTORNEY AT LAW

P. O. BOX 9300
MINNEAPOLIS, MINNESOTA 55440

TELEPHONE (612) 475-6357

June 20, 1988

Mr. Jim McDougall
3415 The Mall
Minnetonka, Minnesota 55345

Dear Jim:

    I was out of town and missed your Cargill send-off, but did not want to let more time go by without wishing you well on your retirement.

    I also want to acknowledge and thank you for your patience and courtesy and friendship over the years that I represented Nutrena. The Law Department and I, in particular, made a lot of demands on you. I hope you realized that my frequent requests for assistance reflected my respect for your judgment and experience and ability to teach even lawyers what end of a steer does what.

    I hope you will stop in upstairs when you visit Nutrena from time to time, and that your retirement is as exciting as (but much less stressful than) practising feed law part-time with Cargill.

                                Yours truly,

                                H. Jed Hepworth

HJH:ds
pl/4024

Jed Hepworth's letter on the occasion of my retirement, 1988. Courtesy of Cargill, Incorporated.

in the first place. This in turn helped save much valuable time, which is such a large part of those losses. However, despite our best efforts to combat and prevent those litigious situations, some still came to fruition.

Our Feed Division was occasionally involved in lawsuits even though we had the competent services of our top corporate lawyers, who worked with us and were partially responsible for Feed Division litigation. I was requested on several occasions to explain to juries the intricacies of ruminant digestion and how related factors might cause or prevent livestock losses from happening.

It was very gratifying to me to receive a letter upon my retirement in 1988 from our law department representative, Jed Hepworth, expressing appreciation for our successful working relationship.

Another part of our business that required a good share of my time was the responsibility of making sure that the Caprock Division stayed at peak performance in the industry and that it was competitive, profitable and free of problems. This involved keeping Caprock up-to-date on rations that produced most low cost gains and making sure that its health programs and nutrition programs fit together optimally to produce the results that would keep customers coming back with more and more cattle in order to keep the Caprock feedyards full.

The representatives from Caprock Industries were not totally satisfied unless I was investing all the time that they felt was required to serve their best interests and to help them prosper.

Cargill's Mission and Values

Helping the world thrive: "Our purpose is to nourish the world in a safe, responsible and sustainable way. Every day, we connect farmers with markets, customers with ingredients, and people and animals with the food they need to thrive. We combine our experience with new technologies and insights to serve as a trusted partner for food, agriculture, financial and industrial customers in more than 125 countries."*

I really appreciated the ethical values that Cargill espoused across the board. First and foremost was the understanding of how important it was to develop a high level of trust. There was a tremendous emphasis on integrity and honesty. Cargill operated much like the cattle feeder himself, whose word was his bond. The cattle feeder did a lot of business on a hand shake, and Cargill

---

*— Cargill's mission as stated on www.cargill.org.

Chapter Three: My Career with Cargill

Being interviewed in 2016 by Bruce Bruemmer, Director of Cargill's Corporate Archives, to share historical perspectives about the evolution of the beef feed industry. Courtesy of Cargill, Incorporated.

employers and employees proved that they were true to their word as well.

Cargill took a strong stand against failure to deliver on promises or guarantees, such as not abiding by an agreement, failing to honor a pre-fixed price, or selling a product that did not live up to promised expectations. A prime example was that of honoring the seasonal booking prices for cattle feed that Cargill gave the farmer feeders in advance each fall after the grain harvest. Cargill would

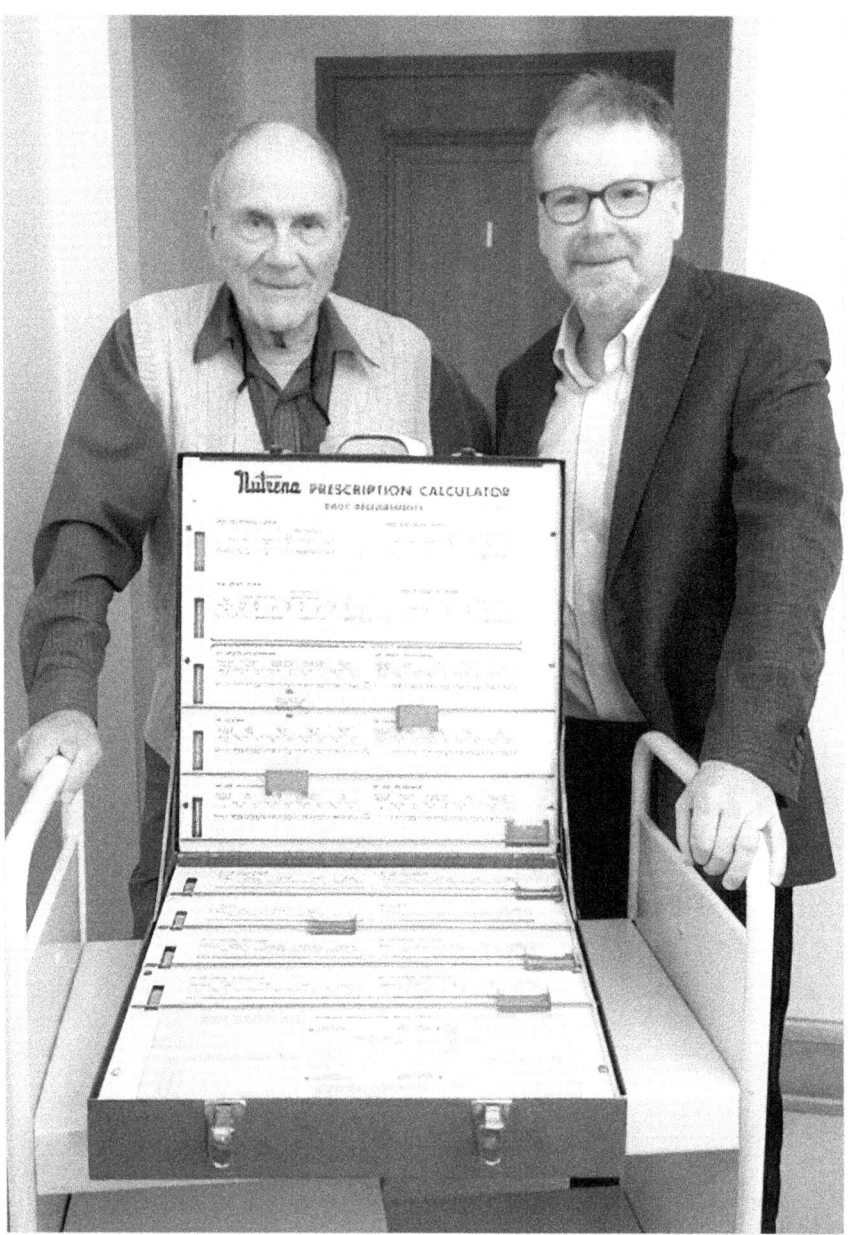

With Bruce Bruemmer by the Nutrena Prescription Calculator. Courtesy of Cargill, Incorporated.

always stand behind their price guarantees, even when the cost of their feed ingredients ended up being higher than expected. Other feed companies, including our top competitor, would sometimes renege on their agreements, but Cargill never did.

Another area that I really admired about Cargill as a company was its emphasis on safety. Cargill wouldn't tolerate anything that was a danger, especially any obvious danger to the employees or customers. Cargill considered anything that could potentially put people at risk of getting hurt on the job to be a cardinal sin.

Finally, I admired the way Cargill used innovative practices to bring the cattle feed industry up to speed with new advances in cutting edge scientific research and technology. Cargill's Research Farm was invaluable in this endeavor. I was very proud to be a part of helping Cargill become a major part of the beef production industry, including developing the Prescription Feeding Program and the Cargill Feedlot System (CFS). These marketing strategies helped introduce science and technology to feed production, thus transforming the animal feed industry. This also proved to be highly effective in increasing our sales. It is gratifying to see Cargill continue to lead the way in terms of innovative developments helping to revolutionize agriculture. To this day, I continue to follow Cargill's pioneering breakthroughs around the world.

Getting It Right

PART THREE: INDUSTRY NEWS ARTICLES

Nutrena Prescription Calculator
New accurate way to check dairy rations

How do you know your dairy cows are getting the right ration? Are they getting the right balance of grain, roughage and supplement to maintain capacity milk production economically?

Ask your Nutrena dealer to check your ration on the Nutrena Prescription Calculator. This business-like machine is part of a new Nutrena service to help you avoid costly ration errors like these:

Too much protein. A ration too high in digestible protein over-stimulates the bacteria in the rumen, creating excess gases composed of valuable nutrients. These gases are eliminated by the animal as wasted nutrients.

Not enough protein. If the ration is low in digestible protein, the rumen bacteria are unable to perform fully their job of helping the animal digest feed. Much of the total digestible nutrients in roughage will pass through the animal as waste.

Not enough T.D.N. If ration is low in total digestible nutrients, cows can't give top milk yields or produce strong calves. Heifers can't put on sound growth. Cows bred for high production may milk well for a short time, but lose weight rapidly, go down in production, have a short lactation.

Vitamin, mineral shortage. A ration without an adequate supply of calcium, phosphorous, trace minerals and vitamins can mean a poor appetite, breeding troubles, low production, a weak calf crop.

Personal ration check
With the exclusive Nutrena Prescription Calculator your Nutrena dealer can readily check rations for your milking herd

Using either the Nutrena Prescription Calculator, pictured above, or the Nutrena Prescription farm book, your dealer can accurately check your ration for correct nutrition and economy. The Calculator is an exclusive Nutrena development and a patent has been applied for.

against known requirements of digestible protein and total digestible nutrients. Quickly and accurately he can help you find out if you are over-feeding or under-feeding protein or total digestible nutrients. It's a personal ration check which helps you get full milk making nutrition out of your own roughage and grain.

Nutrena Dairy Feeds help you keep milk production high, feed cost low

Nutrena Dairy feeds are formulated to meet the dairy cow's heavy nutritional requirements from calfhood through a long, productive adult life. Each Nutrena Dairy feed provides the correct amount of Rumalife for the feeding program it is designed for. Rumalife is Nutrena's special combination of ingredients which promote health, vigor and feed-digesting activity of the rumen bacteria.

For bulk and taste appeal in mixes. Nutrena Sweetflow Bulky is a 12% protein feed with Rumalife, molasses, beet pulp and additional bulky appetite-stimulating ingredients. Sweetflow Bulky is mixed in rations for milking cows, dry cows and heifers.

A complete milking ration with Rumalife. Nutrena Sweetflow-16 is a complete milking ration for feeding with roughage. Contains high quality crimped grains and nutritious Nutrena dairy pellets stepped up with Rumalife.

High-nutrition concentrate. Nutrena Sweetflow-41 Concentrate is a highly fortified concentrate for mixing with grain. It contains generous levels of Rumalife to balance large quantities of grain and roughage.

Special purpose feeds. Nutrena Cattle Wormer is recommended for use on dairy heifers and dry cows for safe, effective worm removal—eliminates need for hand drenching. **Nutrena Rx 560** is an economical, high antibiotic feed for mixing in dairy rations and for use in times of stress. Each pound provides 280 milligrams of aureomycin.

See your Nutrena dealer for mixing formulas using Nutrena Dairy Feeds.

Introducing the Nutrena Prescription Calculator in the mid 1950s. Courtesy of Cargill, Incorporated.

The Nutrena Research Story:

Creative Search For Better Farm Profits

Nutrena's 820 acre Research Farm at Elk River, Minnesota is dedicated to helping farm families increase their income through low-cost production of meat, milk and eggs.

The farm is one of the best equipped private agriculture research centers in the world. The staff includes leading scientists in livestock and poultry production. Large numbers of animals and poultry are kept to carry out the many nutritional and research projects.

As every professional farmer knows, there are literally hundreds of combinations of protein and energy sources, vitamins, minerals, drugs and palatability factors to be considered when formulating feeds. Nutrena takes nobody's word for the right combination, or how much nutrition an animal needs for profitable results. Our scientists find out for themselves.

Before any Nutrena feed is put on the market, it is tested and retested to make sure nutrition, cost and results are combined for maximum profit for the feeder. The swine research project described in the preceding pages is a demonstration of the accomplishments of Nutrena's forward-looking, practical research.

Many other agricultural advances have come from the Nutrena Research Farm. A few of them include: the Nutrena isolation system of swine production; use of a time-lapse camera to record living habits of swine and poultry; the Prescription Calculator system of balancing forage, grain and concentrate for high performance, low cost dairy and beef rations; extensive research on complete cattle feeds; Nutrena Hi-Density system for laying flocks, and many other agricultural "firsts."

Compare Nutrena research with that of any other feed company. Get all the facts. Then let your own honest judgment decide who gives you the most for your money. We believe you'll end up feeding Nutrena . . . and making more money.

Cargill

Nutrena Feed Division/Cargill Building • Minneapolis, Minn. • 55402

Nutrena Research Farm in Elk River, Minnesota. Courtesy of Cargill, Incorporated.

Getting It Right

BIOGRAPHICAL DATA SHEET

8-31-73 (Date)

JAMES Robert Mc DougALL (name)

MANAGER of Feedlot Group & Beef Products Mgr (present title)

BIRTH: (date and place) 12 MAY 1923   LeMARS Iowa

FAMILY: (wife and children) Wife Yvonne MARie   children DANA 27 Betsy 21   JAYNE 19   JACQUELYN 16   SANDRA 13   JAMie 9

PRESENT ADDRESS: 3415 the MALL   Minnetonka MN 55343

EDUCATION: (where attended, year graduated, academic degrees)
Yankton College 1949 BA
South Dakota State University 1951 BS.

EMPLOYMENT: (date you joined Cargill and in what capacity; also list all transfers or promotions and the year)

1951-54 Sulphur Springs Iowa & Hayes Cons Schools AS Vo-Ag Instructor
1954-55 Kingsley School District as Vo-Ag Instructor
1955 Beef Product Mgr Nutrena Div Cargill
1958 Beef & Dairy Product Mgr   "
1960 Beef, Dairy & Hog Product Mgr   "
1962 Northern Regional Sales Mgr   "
1964 Manager of Feed Products & Research   "
1969 Manager of Feedlot Group & Beef Products Mgr

Jim McDougall bio file 1973. Courtesy of Cargill, Incorporated.

Chapter Three: My Career with Cargill

- 2 -

ASSOCIATIONS: (church and civic activities; lodge or club membership; professional or trade associations; offices held)

Methodist Church
University of Minn Board of Directors of Dads Associat,
AFMA
American Cattlemans Association
National Livestock Feeders Ass

MILITARY EXPERIENCE: (dates and theaters of active service; grade or rank held; decorations, U.S. and foreign)

1942 to 1946   U.S. Naval Air Force
AOM 1st Class
Pacific Theatre   Air Medal
2 Presidential Unit Citation

HONORS: (scholastic fraternity; civic or government award; honorary degrees; professional awards; local political offices, elective or appointive)

OTHER:

Jim McDougall bio file 1973, continued. Courtesy of Cargill, Incorporated.

Getting It Right

Feedlot Nutrition and Feeder Attitudes

One gets an overview of Cargill's beef research facilities located just north of the twin cities at Elk River. (Photo Courtesy Cargill Inc.)

Jim McDougall, director of beef programs, glances at his newest revision of the prescription calculator, an accurate feedlot device McDougall has developed for Nutrena dealers to quickly balance rations for energy and protein.
CALF News Photo

Jim McDougall of Cargill Incorporated has stressed nutritional service to both large and small cattle feeders since joining the company in 1955. Consequently, the Minneapolis, Mn., based corporation has been a frontrunner in computer feed formulation and feedlot ration programs.

As director of beef programs for the Nutrena feed division, McDougall is responsible for all dry and liquid products as well as overseer of the beef computer program, CFS (Cargill Feedlot System). This not only entails the training of the many Nutrena territory men across the beef belt but also direct control of four men who are consultants for larger feedlots ranging in size from 5,000 to 50,000 head.

Dr. Carl Alexander, director of beef research and colleague with Jim McDougall in formulating Nutrena's feedlot programs, examines the ration of test presently underway at the Cargill research farm.
CALF News Photo

CALF's major purpose in venturing to Minneapolis to visit with the Cargill executive was to get a first-hand account of how such a major company and one of its key personnel view the nutritional and economic status of the beef industry. How does a company who introduced the computer method of feed blending as far back as 1956 and the computer ration program in 1966 feel about the nutritional progress of the industry and the feeding attitudes of large and small feedlot operators?

According to McDougall the feedlot phase, nutritionally speaking, "has a long way to go. There are still a large number of people feeding cattle who do not know where they are when it comes to sizing up a ration. Most of these feeders do not weigh their feed and consequently feed the cattle differently each day."

McDougall continued by saying that in order for such cattlemen to make an attempt at realizing what they do not know about making a beef animal efficient both cost-wise and nutritionally, they must first be bold enough to buy a feed wagon with scales on it. However, after purchasing the scales the Cargill feed director explained that the next most important step is making sure one knows the moisture of the ration. "Then and only then will these feeders begin to realize how and why it is important to balance a ration for energy, protein, vitamins, etc."

Too many Corn Belt feeders, for example, have listened to or read too many stories about feeding high roughage rations without taking time to closely examine the economics of such a program. In most cases if they would price the roughage ingredients realistically their outlook toward a ratio of profitability and energy would probably change considerably. According to the Cargill executive many of the smaller cattle feeders must get practical about ration formulation and learn how to understand and operate a least-cost feeding program.

With regard to large commercial feedlots McDougall feels that merely being classified as a commercial lot does not signify that this type of lot is doing an above average job of feeding. So far many large lots do not have a complete feeding program or one that they feel comfortable with. For one thing, "there are not enough feedlot managers capable of putting together a workable team. A good manager must be a coordinator and feel confident about relying on proper outside help." A manager who tries to create a self-sufficient lot is not only wasting valuable time but he is passing up expert guidance at little or no extra cost.

Oftentimes this CALF correspondent hears Midwestern farmer-feeders talking about the fact that the large commercial lots in other areas of the nation are in direct competition with them. When asked to expand upon this statement, McDougall called these two groups completely separate facets of the beef industry. For one thing the farmer-feeder is, whether he realizes it or not, a grain producer first and secondly a cattle feeder. For example, "If it is time to plant, he plants." At that time his feedlot program is secondary. The same concept holds true when it comes to purchasing stock cattle. He first harvests his crops then he buys his cattle. A commercial lot on the other hand spends its entire day each and every day, managing a feeding and marketing program for its investors and customers.

Regarding future nutritional research

Chapter Three: My Career with Cargill

FEEDLOT NUTRITION AND FEEDER ATTITUDES

the Nutrena official centered his comments around protein metabolism and the increased utilization of acids. The beef industry stands to learn a great deal more about getting the protein from the rumen into the lower digestive system without degrading digestible protein. Likewise, future acid studies will be directed toward getting the animal to generate more of its own energy. McDougall explained that "Rumensin has opened a whole new area of thoughts and ideas focusing upon these two functions of the digestive, production cycle."

When looking into the future the Cargill director of beef programs, sees the economics of ration formulation headed toward producing more leaner beef meaning less days in the lot. Certain areas of the country will see feedlot rations including more crop residue. In the meantime lots where grain is the primary ingredient available to be fed, will be fed for shorter periods of time in conjunction with an increase in supplementation of feed additives to produce greater levels of energy from the ration as well as from the animal itself. Ultimately, Jim McDougall views grazing as playing a more important role in the total beef program. This will be done by increasing the feeding of grain on grass and carrying cattle to heavier weights on pasture.

(Continued from facing page) Calf News article in July, 1977, describing my role as Nutrena's Director of Beef Programs. Included with permission from Betty Jo Gigot, Editor and Producer of Calf News.

Getting It Right

COWBOYS EYEBALL each animal every day, watching for illness or injury. These are at Leoti, KS.

CAPROCK FEEDLOTS AND FOLKS GROW QUALITY BEEF

Three custom cattle feeding lots in the Panhandle of Texas and a fourth in southwest Kansas are the concern of Cargill's Caprock Industries, headquartered in Gruver, TX.

The operations have a total capacity of 155,000 head — 65,000 at Gruver's two feed lots, 40,000 at Leoti, KS and 50,000 at Dalhart, TX, recently acquired by Caprock.

Young cattle of every breed and crossbreed, weighing between 500 and 800 pounds, are received from ranches in the region and as far away as Montana and northern Mexico.

Some are owned by Caprock, but most are fed on a custom basis for ranchers and other investors. The animals are placed on high-energy rations, formulated by Nutrena Feeds and prepared by mills at each location, for 120 to 150 days. In that time their weight climbs to over 1,000 pounds and they are ready for sale to packing house buyers.

At an average of 130 days per animal, Caprock's cattle population turns over 2.8 time a year, enabling as many as 400,000 fat animals to be finished.

According to Ward Watson, Cargill vice president in charge of Caprock, "The company offers customers expertise in risk management which is rare in the feedlot industry. Cargill's background in commodity futures trading enables it to hedge against undue loss the large amounts of grain we need to feed cattle. We also use fat cattle futures to minimize price risk inherent in ownership of cattle inventory."

Caprock Feedlots description. Courtesy of Cargill, Incorporated.

**CARGILL
NUTRENA FEED
DIVISION**

Nutrena Feeds

Dear Cattle Feeder:

You are invited to attend the Cargill-Nutrena Feedlot Seminar at the Marina Inn in South Sioux City on August 7, 1980. We will have coffee ready for you in the exhibit area starting at 9:45 a.m. Our regular program will start promptly at 10:15 a.m.

This seminar will feature important and proven systems for managing cattle feeding operations:

    * Managing rations for maximum starch digestion
    * Research results with Top Beef
    * Managing bunks and rations
    * Beef Price prospects and pitfalls

James R. McDougall

There will be a panel of specialists to answer your questions in their specific field.

We will also have a full-fledged exhibit area complete with machinery of vital interest to cattle feeders.

Dr. Al Wesley

We will have an excellent beef lunch for you to enjoy at noon, and in addition, we are planning to offer you a chance to win some mighty nice prizes. There will be a set of coupons for you at the door when you register. The coupons are redeemable for products that you may or may not be using now but that can be helpful to you in your feeding operation.

This is an event you won't want to miss, so mark your calendar now and plan to attend. Check to see which other cattle feeders have been invited and plan to attend. You can all come together.

Sincerely,

James R. McDougall
Director, Cattle Feed Programs

Dr. Carl Alexander

Dr. Bill Wheeler

Bob Lewis

Steve Smola

Invitation to Cargill Nutrena Feedlot Seminar in South Sioux City in 1980. Courtesy of Cargill, Incorporated.

Getting It Right

BIOGRAPHICAL DATA SHEET   7/7/82
                              Date

Name: Jim McDougall

Title (VP, AVP, Mgr.): Director Cattle Feed Programs

Division/Department/Location: Feed Marketing Minneapolis

RESPONSIBILITIES OF NEW/PRESENT POSITION:

Responsible for dry beef feed products for Feed division
"   "   Cargill Feedlot Group for Feed division
"   "   Oprock technical advice on Rations + cattle management
"   "   Cargill Feedlot System (CFS)

BIRTH: (Date and place) 5/2/23 Le Mars, Iowa

PRESENT ADDRESS: 3415 The Mall Minnetonka, Minn 55345

FAMILY: (Spouse's and children's names) Spouse Yvonne
Children Donn, Betsy, Jayne, Jackie, Sandy, Jamie

EMPLOYMENT: (Date you joined Cargill and in what capacity; also list all transfers or promotions.)

Month/Year	Job Title	Division/Location
7/1/55	Beef Feed Product Manager	Feed Floor Exchange Mpls
7/1/62	Northern Region Sales Manager	Feed Floor Exchange Mpls
7/1/65	Manager of Research and Products	Feed Mpls
7/1/68	Director Cattle Feed Programs	Mpls

Jim McDougall bio file 1982. Courtesy of Cargill, Incorporated.

Chapter Three: My Career with Cargill

BIOGRAPHICAL DATA SHEET/2

EDUCATION: (Where attended, year graduated, degree/majors)

Westmar College, LeMars Iowa
Yankton College, Yankton SD, B.A.
South Dakota State University, Brookings, B.S.

ASSOCIATIONS: (Church and civic activities; lodge or club membership; professional or trade associations; date offices held)

Methodist Church
National Cattlemens Ass.
Plains Nutrition Council
Future Farmers of America P/C Liste

HONORS: (Scholastic; civic or government awards; professional awards; political offices, elective or appointive)

HOMETOWN NEWSPAPERS:

LeMars Sentinel, LeMars Iowa
Minnetonka Sun
Minneapolis Star Tribune

Jim McDougall bio file 1982, continued. Courtesy of Cargill, Incorporated.

Getting It Right

COWFOLK GATHER AT KEARNEY AGAIN THIS YEAR

More than 350 Nutrena customers — feedlot operators from Nebraska, Iowa, Kansas, Colorado, Oklahoma, Minnesota, South Dakota, Illinois, Texas and New Mexico — were Cargill's guests at the annual Cargill Feedlot Seminar at Kearney, Nebraska, March 2 and 3.

Also attending were 10 newspeople, representing *Beef, The Farmer, Drovers Journal, Nebraska Farmer, Calf News, Kansas Stockman*; Nebraska radio stations KRVN, Lexington;

KMMJ, Grand Island, KGFW, Kearney, and a Kearney television station.

In two days of study sessions they heard from Economists Jim Riley and Dave Petritz about the economic outlook for cattlemen and the effect on cattle numbers of the government's Payment-in-Kind (PIK) program. They also heard a former secretary of agriculture, Dr. Earl Butz, on the theme, "The Name of the Game is Profit."

A panel of four leading feeders presented "Alternatives in Feeding" and an official of the Food and Drug Administration discussed "Chemical Contamination Prevention." Nutrena people presented a skit called "Hiring Practices of the Hardly Able Cattle Company," followed by Gene Sprinkel of Cargill's Excel Corporation who spoke on "Effective Hiring Practices."

CATTLE FEEDERS, all users of the Cargill Feedlot System, check in at the Ramada Inn for two days' entertainment and instruction, guests of Cargill.

ROAST BEEF was main course at poolside dinner, above right.

PROGRAM'S PLANNER, Nutrena's Jim McDougall, welcomes feeders and newspeople to the 10th annual study session.

Cargill Feedlot Seminar in Kearny, Nebraska, mid 1980s. Courtesy of Cargill, Incorporated.

Chapter Three: My Career with Cargill

Cargill People

December 7, 1984

Jim McDougall, Cattle Expert, Markets Feed

There are four McDougall brothers working for Cargill. One's a cattle buyer for Excel. One's a Feed Division territory manager. Another operates a Cargill feed and seed dealership in LeMars, Iowa, the McDougall's home town. And the fourth, Jim McDougall, works here in Minneapolis as a Feed Division product manager.

To round out the picture, there are a couple more McDougall brothers "working for the competition" as cattle buyers for Iowa Beef.

Jim, too, is a cattle specialist. He came to Cargill in 1955. "Commercial cattle feed was not a big factor in the feed business at that time," Jim explains today. But feed additives and scientifically formulated feeding programs were rapidly being developed. "The company recognized that it was going to need someone with expertise in that area," he adds.

As early as 1956 Nutrena had developed a prescription calculator still in use today (though it's revised as new products and information come along). Jim describes the calculator as more than a selling tool. "It's a management tool." Sections of the calculator are devoted to an animal's nutritional needs at various stages of development, to nutritive values in feeds that the farmer has on hand (such as hay and corn silage) and to nutritive values in various Cargill feed products. Using the calculator a Cargill territory manager can show the farmer what Cargill products, used as ration supplements, will provide economical weight gains and give the farmer a good picture of what weight gain and feeding period he might expect.

For major producers equipped with weighing facilities an even more sophisticated program is available. It's called the Cargill Feedlot System. A territory manager's call to the Office Center, with information about a specific producer's cattle weight and available feedstuffs, results in a customized feeding plan, developed on the spot,

(Continued on page 3)

Providing practical, up-to-date information to sales people and producers alike is an important aspect of marketing in the Feed Division. Shown here is Jim McDougall, cattle/feedlot product manager.

Article in Cargill's Exchange Newsletter about my job as Cattle Expert and Feed Division Product Manager, 1984. Courtesy of Cargill, Incorporated.

Getting It Right

Jim McDougall, Product Manager *(Continued)*

using a computer program. Cargill services more than 1,000 major producers with this program.

It's all part of an effort to make the Feed Division's sales force the most expert in the business. "We call them 'masters of beef,'" Jim explains. "We want to equip our sales people so that they're the most knowledgeable, best qualified experts in their area. When local producers seek them out for information about new developments, or ask their advice, our people have a real head start on the competition."

That means training programs and support for sales people in the field are an important part of Jim's job.

Earlier this month, for example, he conducted a week-long training session for 18 sales people, most of whom had been with Cargill for only a few months. "Some of our territory managers come straight from college campuses, where they've had academic training in animal nutrition. Others have come to Cargill from another feed company. In either case, they need to become familiar with Cargill products and the Cargill system," Jim observes.

For sales people back on the job, help from Jim is just a phone call away. He estimates that he gets ten to fifteen phone calls a day, some just requests for additional information, others requiring him to do a little "troubleshooting." Here are some "real life" examples:

— "I have a producer who wants to feed corn gluten feed to his cattle. How much can he feed and do an economical job?"

— "What ration should we feed if we want to limit the amount of grower ration fed to small cattle?"

— "I have a prospect whose cattle are bloating. How can we solve his problem?"

Though the Feed Division has a decentralized approach to management, with 24 districts throughout the United States, Jim concentrates his efforts on parts of the country where cattle are an important factor. "If a guy's doing 90 percent of his business in swine products, I'll leave him alone," Jim reports. But he works closely with sales people in Iowa, Kansas, Nebraska, Texas and other areas in which cattle feed products are a significant part of Cargill's feed business.

Kearney, Nebraska, is the site of an annual event which has proved a great favorite over the years. Producers using the Cargill Feedlot System — and their spouses — are Cargill guests for a period of 24 hours. At the heart of the gathering is a carefully planned seminar. As Jim explains, "Each year when we plan the program, we first determine what subject matter would be of high interest. This depends on pertinent general cattle feed opportunities or problems. Then we decide who can best convey interesting, useful information about that topic to our audience. Then we try to line up that particular speaker. Of course, we have to make other arrangements, too. We send invitations, line up meeting rooms, make hotel reservations and that kind of thing."

In addition to the seminar itself, the producers have a chance to talk to one another. That's important, too. "They talk the same language," says Jim. "In this business we talk about things like 'megacals,' and the producers understand one another."

It's Jim's experience that producers gain respect for Cargill as they meet other big producers with whom Cargill does business. Cargill is perceived as a progressive, innovative factor in the feed business, not just a company following along on other companies' coattails. Members of the press report on the Kearney gathering, and these articles leave a similar impression.

Another, "quite different" program is held in Sioux City each year for Cargill customers and prospective customers.

Yet another aspect of Jim's job is to formulate all rations for Caprock Industries, a Cargill subsidiary that operates four large feedlots in Kansas and Texas. Jim says simply that "Caprock has the reputation of doing one of the most outstanding jobs of feeding cattle of anyone in the industry."

Despite these varied responsibilities, Jim says that the biggest part of his job is developing a master marketing program each year and seeing that the plan is executed on schedule. Marketing goals and objectives are set for each product in his area: dry feeds, controlled release liquid supplements, silage additives. A calendar is developed and followed, to see that certain information about products and programs gets to the field when it's needed. The calendar, naturally, is different for different parts of the country.

Each year's marketing plan emphasizes improved products and programs as well as knowledge and service. "In today's better feedlots, cattle gain is 33 percent faster, and the

(Continued on next page)

Article in Cargill's Exchange Newsletter about my job as Cattle Expert and Feed Division Product Manager, 1984. Courtesy of Cargill, Incorporated.

Chapter Three: My Career with Cargill

Jim McDougall *(Continued)*

time to get cattle to market is 33 percent shorter, than the standard of the industry 30 years ago," Jim reports.

Cargill research has played a major role in developing products and feeding programs that combine new developments from basic academic research with practical, useful feeding methods. Jim emphasizes that "Cargill field sales people convey these programs to the beef producers. That's what scientific progress in animal production during the past 30 years has been all about." Jim McDougall has played a role in that progress.

Article in Cargill's Exchange Newsletter about my job as Cattle Expert and Feed Division Product Manager, 1984. Courtesy of Cargill, Incorporated.

Getting It Right

Nutrena Feeds

SPOTLIGHT

FOCUSING ON SALES AND SALES PEOPLE

November 6, 1987

The Spotlight is published for employees like TM Bob Baylor*, a first time President's Club winner from Stockton district. Bob is in his 7th year of service.

... from Beef Product Manager Jim McDougall

It is encouraging for us in the Feed Division to know that the man who holds the top job in Cargill is a cattle raiser and has many of the same type of opportunities and problems as the prospects that you are calling on.

In addition to his responsibility as Chairman of the Board of Cargill, Whitney MacMillan is also the owner operator of a beef cattle ranch in the big sky country of Montana. Consequently he knows that he needs a live calf from each cow every year. He has also learned that unless ranchers are following a prearranged plan that there are times that critical dates can slip by unnoticed.

Whitney says that some ranchers he knows maintain that they do their work according to the weather at hand and since they are unable to tell what the weather will be they cannot plan out their work, and just thinking like this can be counter-productive to sound planning.

Whitney is enthusiastic about what the Live Calf Calendar can do to help his ranch maintain schedules for management of the tasks and events that must be timed correctly to achieve that live calf from every cow each year.

The Live Calf Calendar can convey constant communication of the critical ranch schedule. It can inform the people of what tasks are to be carried out, who is responsible for that task, why it is necessary and, in many cases, how to do it.

It is a management tool that every good ranch should be able to make use of.

Whitney indicates that he is interested in following up on the success of this exclusive Cargill management tool.

Whitney MacMillan expressing his opinion of the Nutrena Live Calf Calendar to Jim McDougall.

With Whitney MacMillan discussing the Nutrena Live Calf Calendar. Courtesy of Cargill, Incorporated.

Chapter Three: My Career with Cargill

The Science of Feed

Cargill's entry into the feed business demonstrates its early aspiration to be a technology leader in food and agriculture.

BY BRUCE BRUEMMER

Research was the selling point in this advertisement from the 1960s.
Above right: The Nutrena Prescription Calculator in the field.

"YOUR CHICKENS WILL LOVE IT, just watch 'em grow. So feed plenty of it, the cost is low."

These were the lyrics of a radio advertisement that Cargill used to sell Nutrena® feed in the 1950s—a tune some people may still remember. But the company didn't just rely on catchy jingles to sell products. Even before Cargill acquired Nutrena in 1945, it had turned to science and technology to bring value to its customers.

The U.S. feed industry didn't start with the idea of integrating science into the care and feeding of farm animals. Science began to influence animal nutrition prior to World War I with the establishment of farm bureaus and agricultural extension services, but the feed industry tended to rely on salesmanship over science until well after World War II.

In 1957, Cargill embraced the science of feed production when it opened its Research Farm in Elk River, Minnesota. It built on the work of Nutrena Mills, one of the first in the industry to establish a commercial feed research farm in 1937.

Nothing illustrates the shift to science better than Cargill's move into cattle feed. Jim McDougall joined Cargill in 1955 as the product manager for beef feed. In an interview for the Corporate Archives, he described the risks of feeding young cattle the wrong mix of ingredients. "Because of the digestive system, if you put too much energy into that rumen when they are just starting out, the cattle will develop lactic acidosis, and if they get that bad enough, they are crippled," he said.

In order to guide producers to the right balance of feed ingredients, McDougall designed the Nutrena Prescription Calculator in the 1950s. Using it, a Cargill salesperson could dial in characteristics of cattle and their feed, and it would tell the farmers what other feed ingredients should be added to the cattle's daily diet.

Contained in a large metal box, the technology was anything but sleek. In spite of the bulk, it reduced the time needed to formulate feed diets. "I thought it would be great, rather than working on a whole desk full of papers," said McDougall, recalling how the efficiency impressed people. Later on, more portable versions of the calculator were developed.

The technology still needed to be sold, and Cargill provided education. The company sponsored seminars for feedlot operators and training workshops for feed dealers and personnel. At some workshops, they used an actual cow's stomach, preserved in resin, to demonstrate how cattle digest feed. McDougall recalled, "It was such a monster to pass around. However, it was really a great way to demonstrate the working of rumen."

Who says science can't be enhanced with a little showmanship?

Science of Feed Cargill Article in 2018. Courtesy of Cargill, Incorporated.

Getting It Right

CARGILL INTERNAL MEMO

April 19, 1988

To: Lloyd Whiting
         Director of Research and Marketing

From: Jim McDougall

As per our earlier discussion I have compiled a list of activities which I recall being involved in over the years I served with the feed division. This is a list of products and programs that either I originated or was the driving force on the team to establish them in the market place and/or training the salesforce to sell in the market. Some of these you may have trouble remembering, some have been picked up industry wide and many are still being used actively by the field salesforce today.*

I have broken down the products programs and accomplishments into sections based on the various titles that I have held between 1955 and 1988. If there are any questions involving these topics please let me know.

I have held the following positions in the Cargill Feed Division Marketing Department: (according to personnel records.)

Hired July 1, 1955
National Product Marketing Coordinator (for beef).

September 1, 1957
Promoted to National Product Sales Manager (all products).

July 1, 1962
Regional Sales Manager, Northern Region:
   Nebraska, North Dakota, South Dakota, Wisconsin, Iowa and Minnesota.

October 16, 1964
Manager of National Feed Products.

February 1, 1970
Manager of Feedlot Department and Feedlot Group.

* means it was either picked up as a standard of the industry and/or is still active with todays field salesforce.

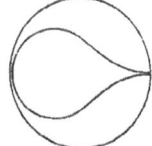

Jim McDougall bio file from 1988. Courtesy of Cargill, Incorporated.

Chapter Three: My Career with Cargill

Page 2

August 1974
Technical Consultant for Caprock Industries.

February 16, 1975
Given added responsibility as manager of all beef feed products.

June 1, 1988
Retired from Cargill at age 65.

July 1, 1955 to September 1, 1957
* 1. Prescription feeding program for beef cattle and sheep.
  2. First Nutrena cattle wormer(phenothiazine) 6.6.
* 3. Rx560 first Nutrena product developed as a blender to be used with concentrates in cattle rations.
* 4. Developed the Rumalife and digestive system story.

September 1, 1957 to July 1, 1962
* 1. Prescription feeding program for dairy cows.
* 2. Calfloo Isolation system for dairy calves original hutch system.
  3. Sweetflow 41 Dairy Concentrate-1st Nutrena high urea dairy concentrate.
* 4. Sweetflow 13 Dairy Pellets-1st Nutrena complete dairy pellets.
* 5. Sweetflow 16 Dairy Pellets-1st Nutrena complete dairy pellets.
* 6. The Nutrena Prescription Calculator.
* 7. 12% cattle fatner pellets program.
* 8. Beefcake 20 and 30 Breeder program. That established Nutrena in Nebraska range feed biz.
  9. Rotating-overlapping swine additive program (antibiotic and chemical additives).
* 10. The three stage sow program.
  11. Sow 15 and Sow 38 feeds.
  12. Special purpose hog concentrates: Shoat 40 A.R. (appetite regulator) Shoat 40 M.C. (mixing concentrate).
* 13. Shoat 40 MCM (Mixing Concentrate Meal).
* 14. Introduced the protein energy egg feed concept with 41% poultry concentrate-along with Dave Wentzell who headed Memphis project to capture independent egg producer business 1962.

July 1, 1962 to October 16, 1964
  1. Helped engineer and execute most successful acquisition of feed company up to that date (Lauhauf Grain "Victor Feeds") retained 90% of the desired dealers and feed business.

Jim McDougall bio file from 1988, continued. Courtesy of Cargill, Incorporated.

Page 3

2. Doubled number of large dealers in Northern Region and increased the business 68% during 27 months service as Northern Region Sales Manager.
3. Had assistance of bright aggressive young salespeople such as Territory Managers, John Seward, Jim Bassett and Sales Trainee Lloyd Whiting.

October 16, 1964 to February 1, 1970
1. Assigned the responsibility for the Nutrena Research Farm. (1964 to 1968).
2. Extruded dog food manufacturing product and sale.
* 3. Prescription feeding programs for horses.
* 4. Horse Kwik Concentrate, Horse Kwik Ration, Horse Kwik-13.
5. Beefcake 50 Block. 1st block from Nutrena Formula.
* 6. Start Kwik and Kwik 2 starting program.
7. High fat vealer program.
8. Preshoat 38.
* 9. Introduced CLS & CLS Cont. Rel.
* 10. Beef Kwik-18 program.
* 11. Dairy-Beef program.
12. Pig-38.
13. The Prime-X Program for cattle.
* 14. Finalized version of Nutrena Pork Production system. (One of most popular hog raising system).
* 15. 12:12 Mineral Livestock Mineral Mixing Mineral.
* 16. The Cargill Feedlot System.
17. Feedlot 631,632,633,634. Feedlot 741,742, 743,744.
18. Was given the assignment of putting together and heading up the "Cargill Feedlot Group"--Mission-- "establish Cargill feeds in cattle feedlot business." At high point had 35 large feedlots on program.

February 1, 1970 to February 16, 1975
1. Supervise feedlot group and help develop commercial cattle feedlot tonnage.
2. Assigned responsibility for all cattle feed products.
* 3. Trained regular field salesforce with feedlot potential to administer CFS program in their assigned areas.
4. Developed new and different type of marketing program for CLS ("Edge of Arctic Ice" movie program) which helped produce peak CLS tonnage of 234,000 tons during 1973-74 crop year (without Caprock).

Jim McDougall bio file from 1988, continued. Courtesy of Cargill, Incorporated.

Chapter Three: My Career with Cargill

Page 4

* 5. Developed Calf Kwik.
* 6. Introduced Beef-Matic feeds and Beef Matic program.
* 7. Developed the beef antibiotic premix line.
* 8. Hired members of feedlot group and gave them training necessary to compete with feedlot consultants.
* 9. Trained the #1 Feedlot Consultant, Dr. Wally Koers, and Top Dairy Cow Consultant, Dr. Mitch Eschebarne.
* 10. Lamb Kwik program.
* 11. Perfected CFS system so that it would perform, better than competitors in commercial feedlots.
* 12. Worked with Hutter and McVay to select commercial feedlots for Cargill's Caprock purchases.
* 13. Developed Feedlot Seminar concept for large feedlot customers and public relations reporters. Organized and held 15 of these seminars in 16 year period over 4,000 attendees.
* 14. Persons put through beef training schools number well over a thousand.

February 16, 1975 to June 1, 1988
1. Officially assigned the task for handling technical responsibility for Caprock recommendations and rations, during which it grew from 64,000 head capacity to 265,000 head capacity. And fed out over 3,500,000 cattle.
2. Named as one of the #8 leading feedlot consultants in U.S.
3. Personally responsible for sale of over 190,000 ton of liquid suspension products to Caprock between 1979 and 1987---also responsible for Nutrena dry feed sales to Caprock (don't have accurate account of tons).
4. Prepared for the Gigot litigation which I feel we could have won as we did all the others tried later.
* 5. Introduced the Top Beef program.
* 6. Developed the "Big Feeder" selling seminar concept, now used successfully at Sioux City.
* 7. Introduced Rumensin feeding programs to field (without a disastrous mishap which happened to others).
* 8. Developed the mineral Rumensin concept for adding to feedlot rations BC-M600 + Min-Kwik Products.
* 9. Developed and introduced the Pasture Plus program.
* 10. Developed the "limited feed" creep feeding program.

Jim McDougall bio file from 1988, continued. Courtesy of Cargill, Incorporated.

Getting It Right

Page 5

* 11. Developed and introduced the original Calf Start Kwik product.
* 12. Trained over 400 people at CFS training schools plus holding 2 advance CFS training schools for over 50 top user salespeople.
  13. During last 2 years feedlot group was in existence 1981 through 1983. It made a district contribution of over $500,000 each year after production cost had been paid to districts for manufacturing the feed.
* 14. Developed new concept of determining cost effectiveness of by-products feasibility in complete type feeds for feedlot rations.
* 15. Assigned as unofficial Future Farmers of America representative and administrator.
* 16. Introduced Doin' Fine Mineral to field salesforce.
* 17. Developed idea of the flowable block beef feeding liquid.
  18. Introduced the "Top Beef Club" to cattle feed customers.
* 19. Developed the "Walky Talky" system to approach feedlot prospects.
* 20. Beef Nutre twins furnishing economics and advantages of compatible dry and liquid supplements.
  21. Have been the feed divisions NCA "rep" since we became charter members of the organization.
* 22. Helped develop and successfully launch the new Haylage-Mate and Silage-Mate products.
  23. Took over product management of CLS products for third time in 14 years.
* 24. Helped develop and launch Doin' Fine Starter program with Nutre-Bio, Doin' Fine Starter Concentrate and Starter Syrup.
* 25. Developed and introduced the Nutrena Live Calf Calendar. Solicited and coordinated funds from 4 suppliers.
* 26. Helped launch the Nutrena poured blocks.
  27. Assisted with litigations and helped win 2 important litigations, one involving over a million dollar claim.

Jim McDougall bio file from 1988, continued. Courtesy of Cargill, Incorporated.

Chapter Three: My Career with Cargill

Page 6

It has been an "action packed" "fun filled" 33 years with many great memories and a few I would just as soon forget.

There is nothing that will help one grow and stay young like working with great people. I have worked with some of the very best.

Sincerely,

Jim McDougall

JM:kkh523

cc: Ralph Grier, Jim Bassett, Dave Larson,
John Seward, Doug Barinsky, Brad Deering
Dick Gosen, Duane Theuninck, John Foley,
Randy Overbaugh, Sue Anderson,
Jed Hepworth, Francis Wingert,
Clarence Whitworth and Dave Wentzell.

Jim McDougall bio file from 1988, continued. Courtesy of Cargill, Incorporated.

Chapter Four:
Family Life

My Wife Von: The Heart of our Family
In keeping with the times, I was the primary breadwinner and was busy working and supporting our large family. Von was content to be a stay-at-home mom during the years our children were growing up, and she was the one who cared for the kids on a day-to-day basis. Von and I were very much on the same page as far as our philosophy of raising children. If we had a disagreement about something, we tried to talk it out and consider each other's perspectives.

For the most part, our kids grew up well-adjusted and happy and stayed out of trouble along the way. Von and I tried to treat them fairly without showing partiality. We

Von and me.

Chapter Four: Family Life

also tried to encourage our kids to develop competence and become independent as they grew. We tried not to interfere with them figuring things out and making decisions on their own, even if we didn't necessarily agree. We had no desire to talk them out of what they wanted to do, as long as what they wanted to do was decent and honorable—and didn't break any laws along the way.

We felt that our kids were likely to grow up and raise their children in a similar manner to the way they themselves were raised, so it was especially important for us to model good parenting. Fortunately, we found that this belief proved to be true, and all of our children have turned

Our six kids at Christmastime, 2001; From left to right: Jamie, Jackie, Jayne, Sandy, Betsy and Dana.

out to be good parents. Von and I were also very happy that, aside from the typical sibling spats and rivalries, our kids got along well together and are still close as siblings to this day.

Our kids describe Von's approach to dealing with them as very loving, gentle and encouraging. She wasn't one to chatter much, but she "walked the talk" and modeled the values she wanted our children to adopt and the way

Von, Dana, and granddaughter Madelyn (age 5) baking cookies.

she wanted them to behave. My granddaughter Madelyn recalls that when one of our kids or grandkids did something that she disapproved of or that she got frustrated by, Von would often be heard to say, "Oh well! Should you throw 'em in the garbage? No, you just gotta love 'em, and love 'em and love 'em!"

My brother Mark shared with us that he witnessed Von in action demonstrating her particular brand of unconditional love and patience one summer when he was staying with us at our Richfield house in the late 1950s. At that time, we still had a milkman, who delivered milk in glass bottles to an aluminum box on our doorstep. Mark recalls that on several occasions, Jayne, who was about five years old at the time, would open the lid to the box and try to pick up the glass gallon bottle of milk. Von would stop Jayne by saying, "Just wait Jayne. That milk bottle is really heavy, and I don't want you to break it. I'll get it." One morning, Jayne got to the milk box before Von could stop her and picked up the bottle of milk. Sure enough, just as Von had warned, Jayne dropped the bottle, which shattered all over the kitchen floor, spilling milk everywhere, including under the refrigerator. Mark remembers cringing and thinking to himself, "Oh no, Jayne's really going to catch it now!" Instead, Von gently scolded, "Now Jayne, you know I told you that you should just wait until I got the milk, because, see what happened?" Mark thought that there would likely have been quite a different response in most other households.

Von's unique brand of gentleness and patience was demonstrated in so many aspects of her life that it would be difficult to describe them all. Jackie recalls one incident when she had made black candles from scratch in our kitchen in Minnetonka. Unfortunately, when she put the candle molds into the refrigerator to cool, she spilled black wax all over the inside of the fridge. It hardened instantly and was very difficult to remove. Von helped Jackie painstakingly chip away all of the wax, and Jackie recalls that during the entire process, Von never scolded her or became cross. When they were finished, Von and Jackie stepped back to survey the cleaned refrigerator, and Von simply remarked. "Just think, Jackie, we spent the whole afternoon cleaning the wax out of the fridge, and everything looks just the same as it did when we started out!" Jackie was obliged to agree.

One day when our children were quite young, I decided that they could use some pointers in social refinement. I took it upon myself to do a little research on the subject, and I purchased a copy of *Emily Post's Guide to Good Etiquette.* I came home and handed the book to Von and suggested that we use it to give some pointers to the kids. Von opened up the book, looked at the table of contents and paged through it. It didn't take her long to hand the

Chapter Four: Family Life

My sweetheart, Von, and me.

Von with our grandson, Shane, at about 9 months old.

Chapter Four: Family Life

Von was known for her kind, gentle and loving nature, shown here again with Shane, about age two.

book back to me, saying, "Thanks, but no thanks." Von had her own ideas about how to convey these same lessons in proper upbringing and good manners. Her approach may have been more indirect and it may have taken longer, but it apparently paid off in the long run, as I am happy to say that our children have grown up to be fine ethical and well-mannered individuals, and I am quite proud of them all.

Von's way of communicating was with humor, empathy and tact. A twinkle in her eye and her winning smile were her trademarks, and her wry Irish wit was often in evidence when she wanted to make a statement or get her message across. She had a knack for putting things in perspective, and one of her favorite sayings was "Everything in moderation." When major challenges arose or when things weren't going well, she would often just shrug and sigh, "Oh well, this too shall pass," or "Don't worry—it's just a stage." She'd encourage the kids to just do their best if they were anxious or worried and reminded them that we would always be there for them no matter what.

In keeping with her kind and gentle nature, Von was a very quiet and unassuming individual who didn't tend to call attention to herself. She preferred putting other people

Von's Surprise 90th birthday party in December 2011.

first. Even though Von didn't usually like being the center of attention or stealing the limelight, it was obvious that she excelled at being a wife and a mother. My son-in-law, Brian, captured Von's essence so well in his eulogy at her funeral service: "I've seen the force of (Von's) love and character silently aligning our family . . . like gravity . . .

Von and I stealing a kiss at The Colony Skilled Nursing Facility after her stroke in 2014.

you can take it for granted, but it is always there, always pulling in the same direction, a constant force bringing everyone together."

Sadly, Von passed away on January 6, 2015, at the age of 93, due to complications from atrial fibrillation and a stroke. One of the most comforting and encouraging thoughts that I have had after losing Von was when my daughters informed me that Von had shared with them that she felt that marrying me had substantially lengthened her life. She said she had had so many enriching opportunities and experiences, such as giving birth to our six children, working in some enjoyable settings, such as Dayton's Department Store and Montessori Preschool, and traveling to many interesting and exciting places.

Our Homes in Richfield and Minnetonka, Minnesota
In 1955, as a result of my being hired to take my new position with Cargill, we moved from Kingsley, Iowa, to Richfield, Minnesota. At that time, our family consisted of Von and me, and our three daughters, Dana, Betsy, and Jayne (ages eight, three, and one respectively). This move constituted a major transition for us since it involved relocating from the small rural town of Kingsley to the large, bustling, rapidly expanding suburb of Richfield, just south of the city of Minneapolis. Von didn't drive, so before the

kids started to reach driving age, if I wasn't around to chauffeur, our family members usually walked to wherever they needed to go. We rented a small two-story house located at 7514 Fifth Avenue South, in Richfield, and settled into the neighborhood along with many other families who had young children. We were very comfortable there for about three years and made good friends with some of our neighbors, including Fred Saltvold, who was to become one of my most valued and esteemed colleagues at Cargill. By sheer coincidence, the Saltvolds happened to live catty-corner to us in the same block of our Richfield neighborhood.

In about 1959, the city of Minneapolis, responding to a rapidly increasing population and expanding metropolitan

Betsy and Jayne in front of our Richfield House in 1959.

Easter Chaos. Betsy, Jackie, Dana, and Jayne in Richfield in 1959.

area, started constructing Interstate Highway 494, which to this day, along with Interstate Highway 694, serves as the major loop that runs around the Twin Cities. While building Highway 494 turned out to be a great move for the city of Minneapolis, it resulted in a major disruption to our family life, as the construction of the road a couple of blocks away from our house caused our very shallow well to dry up. Unfortunately, our landlord was traveling outside of the state at the time, and I was unable to locate him right away and notify him about our well problems. Consequently, we had to relocate in a hurry. Von and I decided to purchase our first home in Minnetonka, a suburb about 15 miles west of Minneapolis, where we ended up spending the remainder of our child-rearing years. Von and I spent almost 25 years of retirement there together, and I still live there to this day, more than 60 years after we moved in.

At the time of our move to Minnetonka (in 1959), Dana was twelve, Betsy was seven, Jayne was five, and our fourth daughter, Jackie, was about a year and a half. Our fifth

Our house in Minnetonka at 3415 The Mall.

daughter, Sandy, was born after our move to Minnetonka on September 11th, 1959, and our only son, Jamie, was born on February 13th, 1964.

In the mid 1970s, Cargill moved their corporate headquarters from downtown Minneapolis to Wayzata, a suburb bordering Lake Minnetonka, about 15 miles northwest of Minneapolis. This ended up being a major stroke of luck for me, because, much as I enjoyed the other members of my carpool, I no longer had to drive 15 miles each day to downtown Minneapolis, facing the rising sun early in the

From left to right, Jayne, Sandy, and Jackie with baby Jamie at our home in Minnetonka in 1964.

morning, and then home 15 miles to Minnetonka facing the setting sun in the late afternoon.

According to their own accounts, our kids grew up in the family-friendly, woodsy neighborhood of Minnetonka, which came to be known as Tonka Woodcroft. They were in good company, having many other kids of similar ages to make friends with, and they spent lots of their free time outdoors, engaging in activities such as: swimming and biking in the summer; raking up leaf piles and making "leaf houses" in the fall; and skating, sledding and building snow forts in the winter. Our kids also played lots of neighborhood games, such as I Spy, Red Rover, Captain May I, Red Light, Green Light, Starlight/Moonlight, Spud, Kick the Can, etc. There were no electronic devices to distract kids in the 1950s and 60s other than the television. In the evenings, after all the homework was completed, we would often enjoy comedy shows on television, such as *Candid Camera*, *I Love Lucy*, *Carol Burnett*, and *Red Skelton*. Every Sunday Von would go to church with the kids, and then prepare a delicious roast beef dinner, which we would eat around 2 pm. On Sunday evenings, Von would take a break from cooking suppers, and we would all watch Walt Disney's *Wonderful World of Color*. Von would lay out a plastic mat in the middle of the living room carpet, where the kids would sit in front of the television and munch on popcorn and apples and drink hot cocoa.

Betsy, Jayne, Sandy, and Jackie (clockwise from top left) ready for a family TV session on Sunday night in 1964.

Chapter Four: Family Life

In our backyard in Minnetonka: (left to right) Dana, Jackie, Betsy, Sandy, and Jayne, about 1964.

My job was to sit on the couch and throw a pillow at the kids' backs during the suspenseful or scary scenes of the television programs to startle them and get them to jump a foot high off the mat.

Von and I considered ourselves very fortunate to be able to take advantage of the excellent Minnetonka school system for our kids' education. Our kids seemed to thrive under the guidance of many outstanding teachers and participated in a wide variety of activities, including Girl

Swimming at the Cargill Pool in 1964. From left to right: Jackie, Dana, Betsy, and Sandy. Courtesy of Cargill, Incorporated.

Chapter Four: Family Life

Jamie in his hockey gear in the mid-1970s. He also played football, baseball and wrestled.

Scouts, Student Council, Candy Striping, and sports such as softball, broomball and tennis, and in Jamie's case, wrestling, baseball, hockey, and football. The kids were also involved in various after-school activities, such as working on the school newspaper and yearbook, drama club, and school theater productions.

Babysitting was a regular means of earning spending money in our family, and our phone was always ringing with requests, especially with five girls living in our home. Both Betsy and Jackie even earned enough money (starting off at 50 cents an hour) for trips to Europe with some tidy sums left over for college. Other typical revenue-generating activities included waiting tables in restaurants, working as store clerks, and for Jamie, caddying at local country clubs.

Our house at 3415 The Mall in Minnetonka wasn't a very large one for a family of eight, and we sometimes found ourselves a bit crowded, especially considering that until the mid-1970s, we only had one bathroom. I usually got up earlier than the rest of the crew to go jogging and was out of the way before the flurry of early morning preparation began for everyone else. The girls claim that they learned a lot of their negotiating skills through taking turns at the bathroom mirror. They also discovered, after leaving home, that they made good roommates because they were in and out of the bathroom in no time flat!

Chapter Four: Family Life

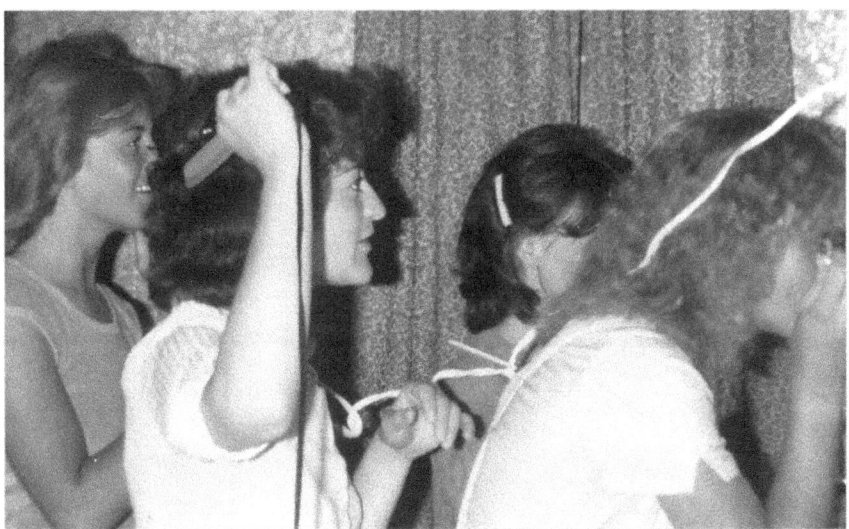

Four of our daughters primping in front of the bathroom mirror before a family portrait.

Von and our daughters all crowded into our tiny kitchen in Minnetonka. From left to right: Dana, Jackie, Jayne, Von, Sandy, and Betsy.

Von was an excellent cook and with the help of our daughters, created her own cookbook which our kids are all very thankful to have.

Chapter Four: Family Life

One of our many Christmas dinners at Dana and Frank's house, 2001.

Our kitchen was also quite small, and much to Von's chagrin, everyone seemed to want to gather in the kitchen and chat while she was busy preparing meals. She was good-natured about the crowded quarters for the most part, except when someone was planted right in front of the refrigerator or the stove when she needed to get things done. We also had a running joke that we had five (girl) dishwashers in our family, but none of them worked!

Another running joke in our family was that we referred to ourselves as "the Circle Family." This is because the kids often seemed to run around in circles when they would be

Getting It Right

Family Portraits at Round Hill near Durand in 2007. Top photo, standing from left to right: Sandy, Jayne, and Jackie. Sitting from left to right: Betsy, Me, Jamie, Von, and Dana. Bottom photo, standing from left to right: Frank, Jayne, Tim, Brian, Jackie, and Len. Sitting from left to right: Dana, Jamie, Lucy, Me, Sandy, Von, Lee, and Betsy.

Me with most of our grandkids and great grandkids, Christmas 2019. From left to right: Madelyn, Samantha, Dani, Emily, Jemma (Jay), Jeff, Julia, Aaron, Angie, Shane, Georgia (Ash), Me, Nick, Cheri, Daniel, Anthony, Zane, Eddie, Ryan, and Jarrid. Not pictured: Erin, Elena, Alden, Ellie, Matthew, Martin, Aidan and Sam.

getting ready to go somewhere and someone would inevitably remark, "We're circling now!"

Thinking back on it, having only one bathroom for eight people might have been part of the reason behind all the "circling." There were many mornings where the kids would run around shouting, "The bus, the bus!" when the school bus arrived before they were out at the stop. And on many occasions after we finally succeeded in rounding up the whole gang in the car to go somewhere, I can remember that someone inevitably announced, "Well, we're off like a herd of turtles!"

The Six Diamonds

Von and I considered ourselves to be wealthy, because we were given some precious jewels to raise. We taught our six children the lesson that there was more than one way to become rich. Von and I thought that every one of our children was a gem, and we referred to them as "our six diamonds."

Our "Diamonds" made Von and me feel as if we were wealthy indeed. By name, they are Dana, Betsy, Jayne, Jackie, Sandy and Jamie. I am proud to report that they

Our family portrait from the mid-1980s. From left to right standing: Jamie, Dana, Von, Jayne, and me. Seated in front: Jackie, Sandy, and Betsy.

Chapter Four: Family Life

Von and me and our six children and their high school graduation pictures. Clockwise from top right: Dana, Betsy, Jayne, Jackie, Sandy and Jamie.

Getting It Right

Me with our six "Diamonds," Christmas 2019. From left to right: Jamie, Sandy, Jackie, Me, Jayne, Betsy, and Dana.

have all grown to be well-adjusted and successful adults and have families and careers that they are proud of. Von and I considered ourselves very fortunate indeed to have six children, seventeen grandchildren and eight great-grandchildren.

I thought it would be illustrative to relate a few anecdotes about each one of our Diamonds as they were growing up, which may shed some light on what our family life was like, and about how each of the kids turned out later in life. All six Diamonds have wonderful families of their own now and are involved in many activities, including being active in their churches and volunteering for their communities. It would take up too much space to describe all of that in detail, so for the sake of brevity, I decided to focus on a few stories about each of the Diamonds when they were very young that foreshadowed their developing personalities and then describe in a nutshell what they ended up doing "when they grew up." By the way, it is interesting to know that the Diamonds have set up a texting thread that they use often to communicate, and which is named "Diamonds in the Rough."

DIAMOND #1: DANA

Dana is our first Diamond. As is true with most parents, in raising our first child, Von and I admittedly faced a bit of a learning curve. And as with most parents, we soon learned how quickly little kids can get into trouble. This held true even for such a charming and well-behaved little girl as our Dana. When Dana was about three years old, Von and I were attending classes at SDSU, and our living arrangements consisted of an expandable trailer with a small yard out back adjacent to another trailer. A little girl named Pitsy lived in the trailer next door to ours, and she belonged to a war veteran and his wife who had met over in Europe during World War II. Pitsy was a year or two older than Dana, who was about four at the time. Pitsy and Dana would often play together in the area between the two trailers. One day Pitsy came over and asked if Dana could play. After a few minutes, Von and I looked out the back window of our trailer and saw Pitsy and Dana sitting on Pitsy's steps. Pitsy had gotten ahold of a large jar of peanut butter, and she was alternately eating spoonfuls herself and then giving Dana spoonfuls. It didn't take long for Von and me to realize that Dana was starting to choke and gag on the peanut butter. Dana's mouth was so full of

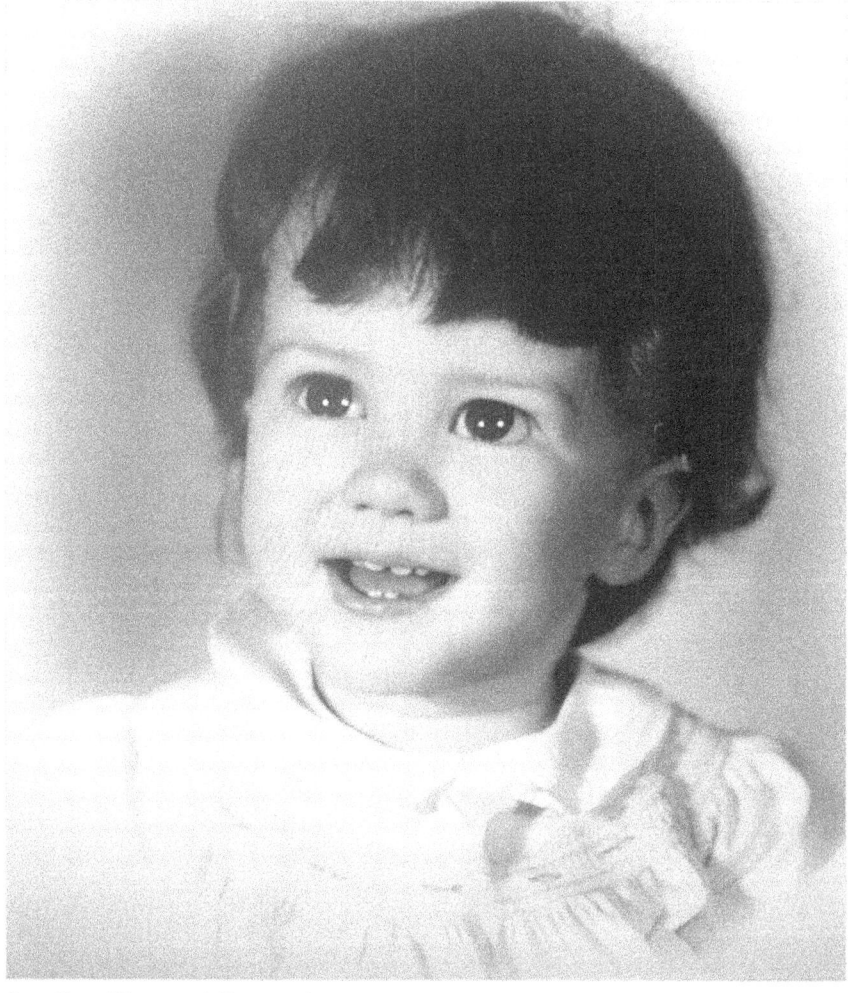

Our first Diamond, Dana, about one year of age.

Chapter Four: Family Life

Dana going to school at SDSU in 1952 at about age five, pictured in front of our veterans housing unit.

peanut butter that she couldn't swallow or talk, and all the while, Pitsy kept shoveling in more and more. Needless to say, Von and I dashed out to save Dana from choking on the peanut butter and quickly began scooping it out with tissues so that she could breathe again!

As we all do as kids, Dana also realized that there was a learning curve to acquiring good manners. She recalls that her preschool made a point of teaching the social graces to their young charges, and students who were guilty of various infractions had to take a time out behind a screen in the classroom. One day, Dana had to "go behind the screen" for a time-out because she slurped her soup. This must have made quite an impression on Dana, because after that incident, she went home and began pointing out minor lapses in manners, such as elbows on the table, to her Mom and Dad. You can imagine how well that went over!

Fortunately, Dana successfully navigated these early "crises," and she went on to become an excellent role model for all of her younger siblings and has led the way with her generosity of spirit and her effervescent charm and vivacious personality. Dana has had a variety of careers over the years, including: working as a flight attendant for Northwest Airlines, serving as an army wife for over 20 years, helping to coordinate the Reno Air Races, and working for a bank. She and her husband, Frank, have hosted many of our family gatherings over the years, and she is widely known for her gracious hospitality. She has also organized many wonderful family trips to places such as Nevada, California, Hawaii, and the Virgin Islands.

DIAMOND #2: BETSY

Betsy, our second Diamond, was our little pack rat. She started demonstrating this tendency at a very early age. When she was about three years old, we left her at my cousin Chet and his wife Eleanor's house in St. Paul, while the rest of the family went to the circus. While we were gone, Betsy was very industrious, managing to collect a

Betsy's fifth birthday, with Dana beside her, at my parent's farm. This picture was taken by my brother-in-law, Bud Scholer, a talented photographer.

small stash of items, such as an empty raisin box, a spool of thread, a thimble, and a handful of rocks, and stowing them under Chet and Eleanor's couch. Later on, Betsy became known for her tendency to "borrow things," and when confronted by someone who wanted her to return the belonging in question, Betsy would protest, "Well, no one was using it!" Fortunately, for the most part, Betsy outgrew this "borrowing" tendency and instead channeled her pack rat habit into collecting books, puppets and toys to use in her career working with young children with disabilities.

Another interesting trait that Betsy had was her way of hyper-focusing. She was a serious student and sometimes would shut herself away in a room for long stretches of time to do her homework. When she was done, she would come out of the room in the evening, needing to expend some pent-up energy and would "harass and tickle" Jayne, who was usually tucked in to bed by then and was trying to settle down to sleep. Von would often have to yell out from her bedroom, "Would you girls please pipe down and get to sleep?!" Needless to say, Jayne was not the one at fault.

Jackie remembers that when she wasn't harassing and tickling her siblings, Betsy could be a lot of fun and was known around our neighborhood for telling spooky ghost stories, leading "night games" in our back yard, organizing

Chapter Four: Family Life

Betsy as queen in a "Queen of the Neighborhood" parade in about 1963.

plays and other intriguing activities such as "reform school," and starting "the Queen of the Neighborhood" parade, where, of course, she appointed herself as the first queen.

To Betsy's credit, once she locked onto something she could accomplish great things. Betsy started out as a speech and language pathologist and then specialized in Early Childhood Special Education. She had a 35 year career helping children with disabilities in a variety of educational settings in Minnesota, Michigan, and Wisconsin and helped bring Four-Year-Old Kindergarten and expanded early childhood mental health services to her community of Eau Claire, Wisconsin.

DIAMOND #3: JAYNE

Jayne, our third Diamond, is our "gentle giant." I say that facetiously, because she is the only tall one in the bunch—which is ironic, given that she was a very picky eater when she was small and seemed to thrive mostly on peanut butter, bean soup, and spaghetti! Jayne has always been on the quiet side, and she had an endearing habit of giggling when she was nervous or unsure. Although Jayne tended to be shy and mostly preferred to stay under the radar in social situations, she could really dig in her heels and raise a ruckus when she wanted to. When she split her chin open at age three on the rails of her overturned wooden rocking chair and had to be taken to the Children's Hospital in Minneapolis for stitches, it took three staff members to hold her down. After the procedure was finished, Von and I were instructed "never to bring her back to this hospital." Fortunately, we didn't have to!

As was common in the 1950s, the nighttime prayer our kids often recited before going to bed went something like this, "Now I lay me down to sleep. I pray the Lord my soul to keep. If I should die before I wake, I pray the Lord my soul to take." Now if you really consider this, to a child, this prayer can be a bit grim and unsettling. Every so often, after her nightly prayers, Jayne would be lying in bed trying to get to sleep and would get to "overthinking" things. Periodically, she would start crying and lament

Chapter Four: Family Life

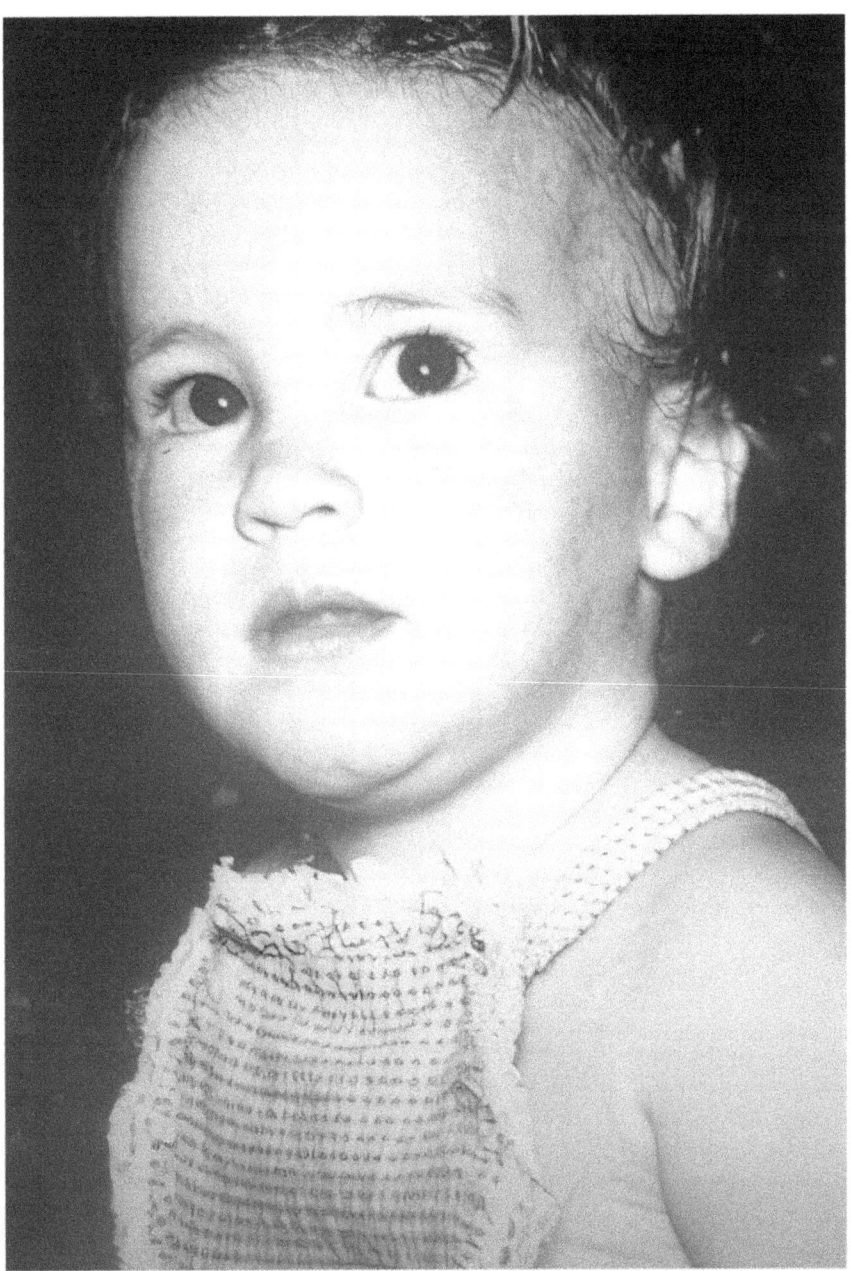

Jayne at about age one.

School portrait of Jayne in third grade.

out loud, "When I die, I don't want to go to Heaven forever and ever!" Von would then come into her bedroom to talk to her and would usually end up asking in exasperation, "Well, Jayne, if you don't want to go to Heaven forever and ever, then where ELSE do you want to go after you die?" With her options clarified in this manner, this seemed to help Jayne put things in perspective and go to sleep.

As is true with many individuals who tend to be more reserved, Jayne is an excellent listener and a keen observer. Von would often compliment her on being our family's best "finder" when objects were missing in our household. In addition, another personality trait that Jayne has cultivated is a strong sense of empathy and caring for those who are sick or injured. Jayne grew up to be a health care provider, and has served as an outstanding nurse in the Twin Cities area for 40 years, specializing in care on hospital medical floors.

DIAMOND #4: JACKIE
Jackie, our fourth Diamond, can be feisty and has always been very good at standing up for herself, yet she is very much of a team player. Jackie is very generous and has a heart of gold.

Jackie's sisters will claim that they have rarely won an argument with her. From the time Jackie was tiny, she

Holding baby Jackie, about 5 months old, in Richfield.

Jackie, age 5, with sister Sandy, age 3.

Chapter Four: Family Life

Jackie's first day of kindergarten.

kept the other neighborhood kids in line with her well-honed assertiveness. Some of her sisters have memories of Jackie at about age three, holding the neighborhood ruffian's chin in both of her hands, looking her right in the eye after she had been guilty of some misdeed, (such as putting Jackie's goldfish in the window well) and giving her "what for," saying, "Now you look here!" Yet Jackie was so kind-hearted and empathetic that she could never even make it through an entire episode of "Lassie" without having to run out of the room to avoid watching the suspenseful climax of Lassie risking her life (which seemed to happen in almost every episode) to save Timmy.

Jackie was by far our most accident-prone Diamond. Von used to say that Jackie's guardian angel would sometimes "fall asleep at the switch," but then her angel would wake up and lay her wings down just in time to catch her. Jackie had many close calls and brushes with disaster, including: being hit by a car, falling down out of a tree house, and fainting and falling off a ping pong table during a bridesmaid dress fitting—losing her two front permanent teeth in the process!

It's a good thing Jackie was so tough and resilient, because she grew up to apply her considerable talents to make many contributions in the world. Jackie became a patient educator, who worked for 25 years at St. Paul Regions Hospital with deaf and hard of hearing clients, specializing in childbirth education and parenting skills. In addition, over the past decade or so, Jackie and her husband, Brian, have hosted a number of foreign exchange students in their home, from countries including Guatemala, Brazil, Spain, Germany, and Italy.

Chapter Four: Family Life

DIAMOND #5: SANDY

Our fifth Diamond, Sandy, is also our fifth girl. Her sisters used to tease her that she was adopted because we didn't have a working camera when Sandy was small, so we had very few pictures of her as a baby or as a toddler. Sandy, with her typical good humor, wouldn't buy that. She would remind everyone that she had figured out early on that if her parents were going to adopt another child, it certainly wouldn't have been a girl, since we already had four of them before she was born!

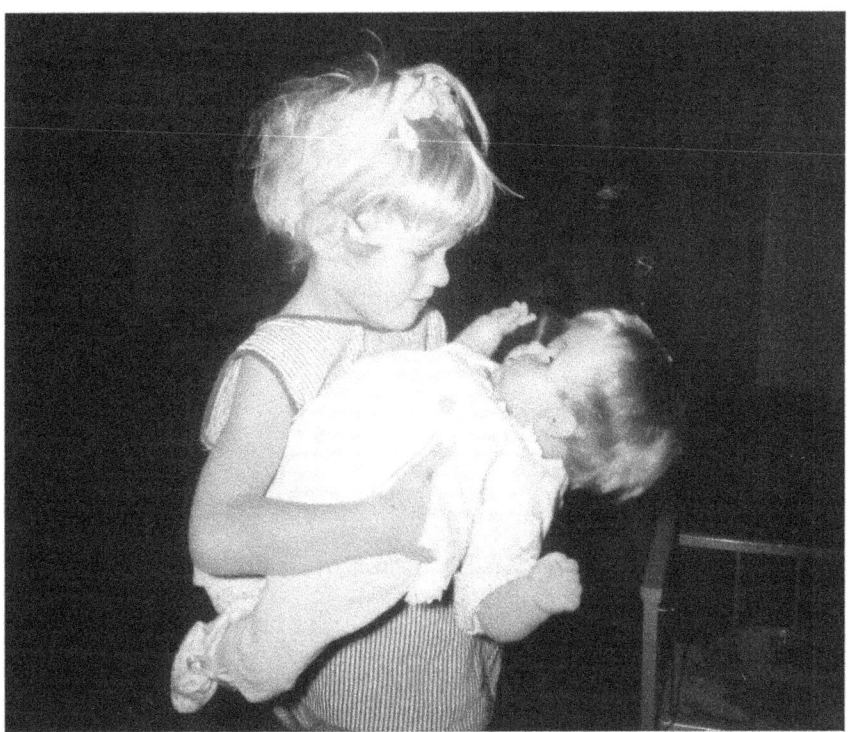

Sandy with her new baby doll at Christmastime 1964.

Since Sandy was our last girl, she was fifth in the pecking order growing up, so she often ended up having to wait her turn behind everyone else. On one occasion during a family trip to Florida, while we were traveling through the deep South, we stopped at a gas station and everyone lined up to go to the bathroom. Sandy was about five years old at the time, and she was a bit apprehensive about flushing strange toilets. Her big sister Jayne, who was trying to ensure that Sandy learned proper restroom etiquette, insisted that Sandy flush the toilet before she came out of the stall and was determined to hold the stall door closed until she did. Unfortunately, flushing this particular toilet turned out to reinforce Sandy's fears, and as Sandy describes it (and she recalls it to this day), "The toilet sucked in the water with a loud 'whoosh' and then started spewing water back out at me, and it wouldn't stop!" Needless to say, having to face this dilemma with the door to the stall being held shut did not help Sandy's fear of flushing strange toilets resolve anytime soon!

Sandy was also known in our family for her sweet tooth. When she was about five or six, after going to the doctor for polio shots with her siblings and hearing all of them complain about it, Sandy offered to take all of their shots for them as long as she could have their lollypops which were handed out after the injections. Sandy's offer was politely declined by the medical staff.

Possibly due in part to being fifth in the pecking order of siblings, Sandy went on to develop some very positive traits, including her patience, kindness, and acceptance of people who face special challenges. One of Sandy's best

Sandy on the new trike she received for her third birthday.

friends growing up was a little girl with disabilities who lived in the next block.

Sandy spent many hours playing with her, and because of their close relationship, Sandy was assigned to be this little girl's "buddy" to help her adjust to school when both of them started kindergarten. In later years, Sandy went on to become a special education paraprofessional for Savage, a suburban school district south of the Twin Cities, and for the past two decades, she has worked with children who have autism and other developmental disabilities.

DIAMOND #6: JAMIE

Last but not least is our sixth Diamond, our only son, Jamie. From early on, Jamie developed as a man's man growing up amongst a horde of adoring females.

This became apparent early on when Jamie was about three. This was in the late sixties, when portable radios were the new emerging "must have" electronic device of the time. While being quizzed about what he wanted for Christmas that year, Jamie announced, "I want a trans-brother radio!" When asked, "Don't you mean a *transistor* radio?" Jamie was quick to insist, "No, I want a trans-BROTHER radio!"

Jamie also had three imaginary friends, "Sam, Charlie, and George," whom he often talked about when he was a preschooler. We think Jamie might have invented these

Chapter Four: Family Life

Jamie at about age two, surrounded by three of his sisters. From left to right: Jackie, Sandy, and Jayne.

three "buddies" to stack the deck a bit more in his favor in terms of our family's boy to girl ratio!

Jamie was at somewhat of a disadvantage early on his life when it came to trying to insert himself into family conversations. At around three years of age, still getting the hang of talking, and finding himself surrounded every night at the dinner table by five loquacious sisters chattering

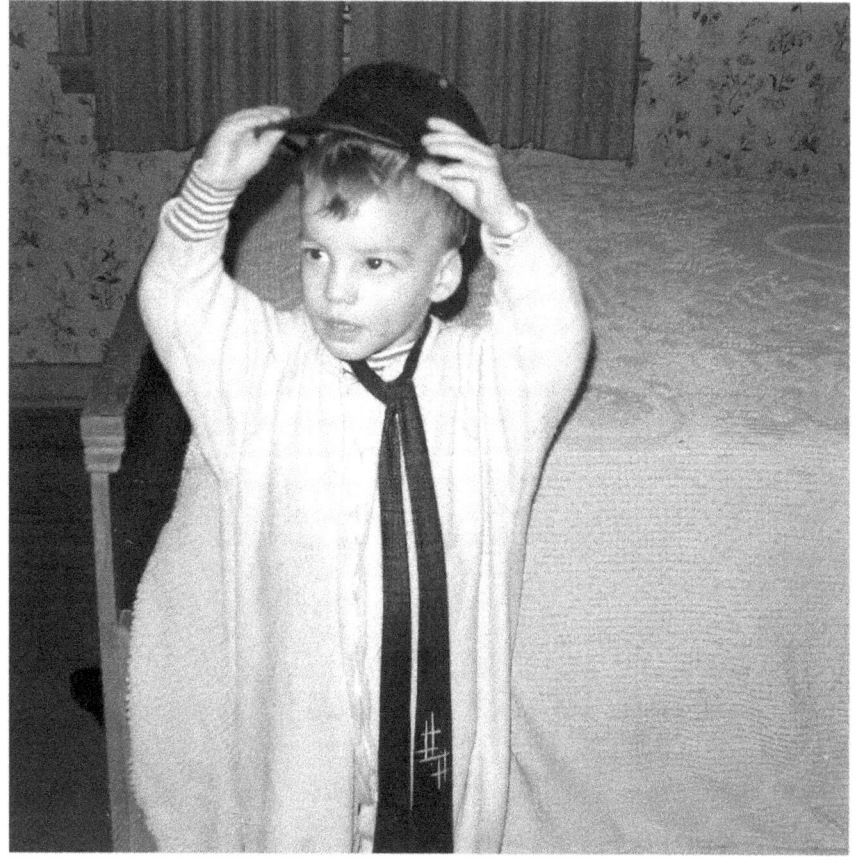

Jamie, about age two, trying on one of my hats and one of my neckties.

Chapter Four: Family Life

away like magpies, Jamie was often hard-pressed to get a word in edgewise. Before long, Von and I noticed that Jamie was starting to stutter, repeating, "I . . . I . . . I" and then appearing to get stuck on a thought, because he had to compete so hard to be heard. We decided to hold a family meeting with the girls, advising them to let Jamie have a chance to talk. For a while after that, it was like that famous commercial on TV, "When EF Hutton talks, people listen," because as soon as Jamie started to stammer "I . . . I . . . I" at the dinner table, everyone instantly froze

Jamie at age three, looking like quite the little gentleman.

the conversation and allowed Jamie to have the floor. The new issue was that Jamie was at a loss to know what to actually say after, "I . . . I . . . I," because he had become so accustomed to being interrupted. So then Jamie started telling jokes. The problem was that Jamie told the same joke every single night, which was: "What do you call a cow that doesn't give milk?" Of course, as we all knew, the answer was "A milk dud." Well, Jamie had a hard time telling us, because he would inevitably crack up before he could get the punch line out.

Jamie went on to develop excellent management and communication skills. He is now Director of Marketing of Companion Animal Products Division at Elanco, where he often speaks in front of hundreds of people.

My Health History

I have been very fortunate to be blessed with good health throughout my life. I attribute much of this to good genetics.

My father, Chet, lived to the age of 80, and my mother, Edith, lived to the age of 94.

Growing up, I did suffer a few illnesses and injuries, but happily I survived them all. Aside from the usual colds and childhood diseases, the first serious illness I remember having was whooping cough when I was around four or five years old.

Chapter Four: Family Life

Then, when I was around eight or nine and was attending country school, I had my tonsils taken out and I bled a lot afterwards, because my blood was too thin. Consequently, I was very weak for a while. Around the same time, I was diagnosed with rheumatic fever. I also had my appendix removed when I was a sophomore in high school and became very ill from the ether that was used as an anesthetic.

The only serious injury I recall was when I was about 14, and I got kicked in the face by a horse. My cousin, Clyde Keough, and I, who were not only cousins but also the best

Out for a buggy ride with my horse, Flash, back in the day. I am the boy in the cart on the far right, and my sister, Mabel, is on my right between the two horses.

of friends, were out riding our horses one day and grazing some of my Dad's cattle along the roadway. I was bending over untangling the reins from the front legs of my pony, Flash. Flash must have touched Clyde's horse suddenly and startled him, because all of the sudden I saw Clyde's horse's hind hoof coming at me. I tried to back away, but before I could, the hoof caught me square in the face. I was very lucky that I didn't break my nose or have any teeth knocked out.

I don't remember any other serious injuries or accidents. I attribute this in part to my dad being very safety conscious with all of us on the farm and putting our well-being first so that, for the most part, my siblings and I avoided serious injuries.

Then while serving in naval aerial combat in the South Pacific during WWII, I developed malaria—three times. (This is described in my book, *Conflict to Combat in the South Pacific,* pages 166-168 and 176.)

Also while in the Navy, I picked up a smoking habit. Then I began smoking more regularly after I was hired by Cargill in the mid-fifties. It seemed everybody smoked in those days. Von smoked then too, but she didn't smoke alone and would usually just have a cigarette or two with me when I came home from work in the evening. I usually smoked a pack a day. The thing that convinced me to stop smoking was that I was starting to wake up with a rattling sound in my chest. I wasn't too concerned the first time or two that it happened, but after a while, I got to thinking, "This can't be too good for me." Also, at that particular time, there was a nationwide public service campaign to increase awareness of the health risks of smoking.

The research findings from credible sources were becoming more and more convincing in establishing the relationship between smoking and lung cancer. In 1964, at about the age of 41, I made up my mind to quit and I never smoked again. Prior to that time, like most people who smoked, I had made several half-hearted attempts to quit, but then would start up again. This time I was serious and I quit cold turkey.

Shortly after I had quit smoking, I was flying out to Nebraska on a business trip, and the flight attendant had just served me a drink. This heavyset guy was sitting across the aisle, and he shook his finger at me and said, "You know, I don't approve of that." He was smoking, and I came right back at him with, "Oh yeah, and I don't approve of what you're doing either." (I had quit smoking by that time.)

Around the time I quit smoking, more and more studies were coming out showing the benefits of regular physical activity, so I decided that I would try exercising on a regular basis to see what happened. I figured that it would be wise to be strategic and follow a well-thought-out plan. First I had to figure out when was the best time for me to exercise. It didn't take long for me to determine that the best time was in the morning before I went to work, and I decided on jogging.

When I first started out, I wasn't very well equipped. I didn't have the right clothing or the right shoes. After I geared up and got into the routine of jogging, I started realizing that I felt better and it was helping me to be healthier. So I had to decide on a jogging route close to home that would become part of my routine. I also needed to figure out how far I should go each day.

My start-up plan involved getting in my car and plotting out my route. I wanted to avoid hills as much as possible. I drove down our street and along a flat stretch of residential road that bordered a marsh. I drove out one mile according to the odometer. Then I turned around and drove back home, and the total of the distance equaled exactly two miles. I started jogging that route every weekday morning. Sometimes I went even further on weekend mornings, but I didn't tend to get up as early.

On weekday mornings, I'd get up at 6:00 am rain or shine, and I'd put the coffee on for Von. I'd get dressed in my exercise clothes and then take the coffee in to Von and set it on the warmer by her bedside, so it was there for her when she woke up.

When our dog, Princess, a Doberman-German Shepherd mix, joined our family in the mid-70s, I started taking her

Chapter Four: Family Life

All set to jog with our dog Princess at Gro-Tonka Park near our house in Minnetonka.

along with me on my morning jogs. She was always ready and willing to go. It usually took me about 25 minutes for my runs—12 minutes out and 12 minutes back. I'd get back home in time to beat everyone else into the bathroom, which worked out well for me, since we had eight people needing to use it most mornings.

I kept up this routine for a long time—from around the time I turned 40 to when I retired at age 65. I seldom missed any days of jogging due to weather, including all through the winter. Over time, I learned to work around the elements. I also would take my jogging gear along with me and would exercise when I traveled on business.

After I turned 65 and was retired, Von and I started going to the Williston Athletic Club religiously—about three times a week. We would swim for 20 to 30 minutes and I would also complete a weight circuit. We were active in this club for about 15 years.

I have no doubt that my exercise regimen prolonged my life considerably. I suspect staying physically active helped Von live longer too. She was a non-driver and was an avid walker throughout most of her life.

Some of my friends and colleagues would give me a hard time about my exercise habits. One of my colleagues started exercising too suddenly and vigorously right after he retired and died of a heart attack in his mid-sixties. Some of my other colleagues wanted to start exercising regularly but didn't really have their hearts in it. And then again, I'm sure some others developed effective exercise programs just as I did.

There is one particular incident that stands out in my mind as especially memorable during my jogging years. I was headed down a road bordering a marsh early one morning with Princess, and I saw this rather large animal that looked like a muskrat running right toward us down the street. It acted disoriented—as if it was confused and didn't know where it wanted to go. I think it might have had rabies. As I lifted up Princess's leash, it ran right between Princess and me. Princess and I both knew that there was something wrong with this particular scenario, and we both stopped dead in our tracks. Then I dropped back and got in front of the animal. I said, "Take it, Princess!" Princess grabbed it immediately by the neck and threw it up in the air. She probably believed she saved the day that time!

At a family reunion with my daughters, who helped me to remain in my home in Minnetonka; From left to right: Jackie, Sandy, Jayne, Betsy, and Dana.

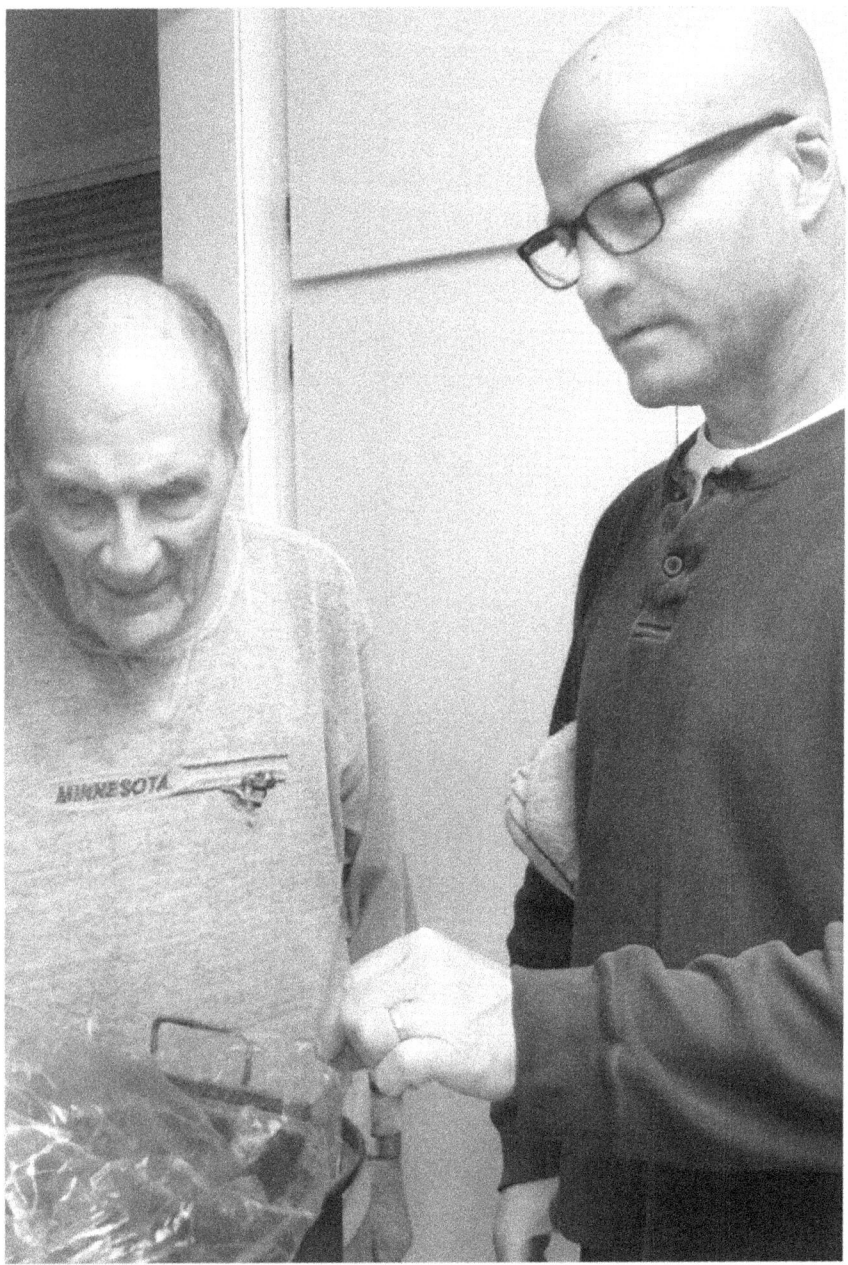

With Jamie checking the Christmas turkey on December 24, 2021.

Chapter Four: Family Life

Throughout my life, I've tried to pay close attention to my family health history and my personal risk factors. When I was around 60 years old, I developed an irregular heartbeat. I was later diagnosed with atrial-fibrillation (A-Fib). Von and I had both been under the care of our trusted family physician, Dr. Donald Pine, for many years, and he told me, "You've got an irregular heartbeat. We'll take care of that." Then the medical staff tried to shock my heart back into regular rhythm. After the shock treatments, my heart did return to a regular beat for a short while, but after a few days, it got out of rhythm again. After two or three weeks of the shocking efforts, Dr. Pine said "We're going to have to look at a pacemaker."

I had my first pacemaker inserted in around 1982, when I was about 60-years-old. Most pacemakers at the time had to be replaced when the battery wore out after several years. The batteries for pacemakers have improved over the years, and I am now on my third pacemaker. I've gotten good mileage out of all of my pacemakers.

I was also diagnosed with stage I colon cancer in 2009 when I was about 86-years-old. I had surgery at the Mayo Clinic in Rochester to remove the cancerous section, and to the best of my knowledge, I have been cancer-free since that time. My dad died of colon cancer when he was 80, and I knew this was one of my risk factors, so I started undergoing regular colonoscopy screenings as I got older.

Reading to three of my grandsons, Anthony, Shane, and Jeff when they were small.

I feel that these regular screenings were the reason that my cancer was discovered at a very early stage.

When I needed surgery for colon cancer in 2009, I wanted to be sure to find the best, most qualified doctor that I could. I asked my family members who work at the Mayo Clinic, Martin and Dori, who was the most sought-after surgeon for colon cancer at the Mayo Clinic and chose my surgeon accordingly. Then about a year after my colon cancer surgery, I developed a double hernia, resulting in weakness in the abdominal wall. I needed surgery for that problem as well, and again, I asked around to find the most qualified doctor for that procedure. I ended up choosing Dr. Dan Dunn, who subsequently became a good friend of mine after he told me that his father had fought in WWII.

Around the time my personal care physician, Dr. Pine, retired in 2008, I started having symptoms of macular degeneration, the dry kind. Over the years, this condition has gotten progressively worse and has made it very difficult for me to read and to locate items around the house, such as television remotes and glasses. I also gave up driving a few years ago because of my vision problems. I live independently in my home in Minnetonka, but I rely on my daughters to take me to appointments, provide meals, run errands etc. I also use adaptive equipment, such as the Topaz Magnifier and voice activated commands with Siri to operate the phone and the television.

With my dear wife, Von.

I am a firm believer in being aware of one's family health history and risk factors, choosing competent and compassionate doctors, participating in annual physicals, following state-of-the art screening guidelines and taking preventive action such as exercising and eating right (including lots of blueberries) to stay as healthy as possible—not just for yourself but for all those you love.

Life started out for me on our farm near Le Mars, a city in northwest Iowa. Here I am as a teenager, standing by a field of corn that was unusually tall by the Fourth of July. The corn then withered on the stalk in the severe drought of 1936.

Chapter Five:
Travel Memoirs

When it comes to travel, I consider myself very fortunate to have had the opportunity to visit so many interesting and exciting places throughout my life. The trips I took enriched my life immensely, and for the most part I really enjoyed the experiences. During the course of my lifetime, I have visited almost all of the 50 states, 17 different countries and 5 different continents. Von traveled to many of these places with me.

Until I joined the Navy at age 19 in 1942, my travel experiences had been quite limited, as I grew up on a farm in Iowa and was busy doing chores with my family and attending school.

The first time I stayed in a motel was around 1933, when I was traveling with my parents through South Dakota, and we stopped in Yankton on the way to Wagner. My dad had some business there finalizing the rent on a farm we were leasing at the time. While Dad was checking on business, my mom treated me to a strawberry ice cream soda at the local drugstore in Yankton. I vividly remember this, because I so seldom had the opportunity to spend time alone with either of my parents. I recall wondering why the drink was called a "soda." I also remember that on that trip there were guys boxing in the middle of the street in Wagner, and this sparked my interest in boxing. I participated in many boxing matches during my teenage years and during my time in the Navy. My interest was also piqued by listening to boxing matches on the radio, especially those featuring Joe Louis, who reigned as the world heavyweight champion from 1934 to 1949.

Then in 1942, early on in my naval career, I was thrust into quite an amazing travel adventure. I believe I have the remarkable distinction of setting a record for the most miles ever traveled to join a naval patrol squadron. It started soon after my enlistment. In the chaos that ensued right after Pearl Harbor when the nation was scrambling to prepare for all-out war with Japan, through no fault of my own, I had missed my squadron's departure from the United States to Australia. These were the days before the Navy routinely used aircraft to transport personnel, and I embarked on an incredible journey of 16,642 miles to

Chapter Five: Travel Memoirs

catch up to my squadron during the months of September and October, 1943. My itinerary was as follows: I traveled 533 miles by train from Chicago, Illinois, to Memphis, Tennessee; then 1,044 miles from Memphis to Miami, Florida; then 960 miles from Miami to Norfolk, Virginia; then 2,967 miles from Norfolk to Oakland, California; and then 7,070 miles by ship from Oakland to Townsville, Australia; and once again by train 4,068 miles across Australia to Perth—for a grand total of 16,642 miles. This was quite a trip for someone who up until that time hadn't traveled beyond a 200-mile radius outside of the family farm!

My 4068-mile Australian route to catch up to my Navy squadron in WWII.

Once I joined up with Squadron VPB-52, I served as a combat air crewman, ordnanceman, and bombardier and flew missions with the Catalina PBY Black Cats in the South Pacific. Our primary mission was to fly night patrols in order to cut the supply line between Japan and their

Photo of me published in *Yank Down Under*, 1944, performing duties on a Catalina PBY.

Chapter Five: Travel Memoirs

PBY Catalina over the South Pacific. This was the type of plane I flew in during WWII.

main base of Rabaul, on the island of New Britain in the Australian territory of New Guinea. This covered an area of about 3000 miles. My story from that period is chronicled in my book, *Conflict to Combat in the South Pacific*.

The next phase of my travels, during the period of 1946 to 1955, was confined mostly to the Midwest. After I was discharged from the service in 1946, I returned to the U.S. and married my fiancé, Von, in my hometown of Le Mars, Iowa. Then I attended college in Yankton and Brookings, South Dakota, from 1946 through 1951. After graduating in 1951 from SDSU, I taught for four years as a Vo Ag instructor in several communities in northwest Iowa, including: Hayes, Sulphur Springs, and Kingsley. Most of my traveling in those days involved driving between these communities to serve my schools, consult with farmers and advise on FFA projects. I also traveled to Sioux City for the FFA Judging Competitions and took periodic trips home to Le Mars to visit my family.

After being hired by Cargill Incorporated, in 1955, I soon began traveling for the company on business trips, starting with a series of brief meetings and consulting sessions. Later on, my trips gradually evolved into Cargill Feedlot Seminars, Regional Feeder Meetings, Marketing Seminars, National Cattlemen's Conventions, National Livestock Feeders, and Nutrena Classes for Territory Managers and Beef Feeders. Some of my consulting trips with Cargill

I was able to travel extensively both during my career with Cargill and also with my family for fun. Courtesy of Cargill, Incorporated.

took me overseas, including to Spain and Jamaica. In the late 1970s and early 1980s, Von began joining me on many of these Cargill business trips, as wives were invited along to join their husbands for select events to encourage more of a family approach to marketing with the salesforce.

In late 1992, shortly after I retired from Cargill, I did some consulting for the ACDI/VOCA Program (Agricultural Cooperative Development International and Volunteers in Oversees Cooperative Assistance) and spent about two months in Ukraine and Poland. Von was encouraged by ACDI/VOCA to join me on this trip. "Since 1963 and in 146 countries, ACDI/VOCA has empowered people in developing and transitional nations to succeed in the global economy. Based in Washington, D.C., ACDI/VOCA is a nonprofit international development organization that delivers technical and management assistance in agribusiness, financial services, enterprise development, community development and food security in order to promote broad-based economic growth and vibrant civil society."*

Vacations and Family Trips

Most of my traveling after retirement was for pleasure. Von and I also traveled throughout the U.S. and internationally.

---

*— acdivoca.org

My family at the Wisconsin Dells in about 1965. From left to right: Sandy, Jackie, Jayne, Dana, Betsy, and Von. Sandy was terrified on this trip because we were walking through "Witches Gulch" on one of the boat trip stops.

As a couple, we visited most of the 50 states and 10 foreign countries.

Some of our more memorable domestic trips included traveling to Alaska, Hawaii, Washington State, Nevada, California, New York, and New England (including Bar Harbor, Nantucket, and Cape Cod). We took advantage of several Elder Hostel Programs, now referred to as the Road Scholar Program. These included: Ely, Minnesota,

Chapter Five: Travel Memoirs

At Story Book Gardens in the Wisconsin Dells; From left to right Jayne, Jackie, Dana, Sandy and Betsy.

Sedona, Arizona; and several National Parks, including Glacier.

Our international trips included Ukraine and Poland, Australia, Canada (Banff, Lake Louise, Jasper, Thunder Bay, and Vancouver), England, Scotland, Ireland, Mexico (Puerto Vallarta, Mazatlán, and Guadalajara), the Bahamas, and Jamaica.

We also went on numerous family trips both before and after retirement. As our kids got older, Von and I made a

Vacationing with Von in Jamaica in the 1970s.

point of taking them on an annual road trip to such places as New York State, Florida, Georgia, the Ozarks, Colorado, and all around the Midwest. We wanted to show our kids that the world was a lot bigger than their small village of Minnetonka and to introduce them to a love of travel and adventure. Von and I bought a camper in 1972, and our family frequently stayed in campgrounds in northern Minnesota, Wisconsin, Iowa, and Kansas. The furthest places we took the camper (all in the early 1970s), were:

On one of our family's trips with the camper to Colorado. From left to right: Jamie, Sandy, Jayne and I.

to Pueblo, Colorado, to visit Von's sister, Gerrie Allen; to Estes Park and to the Rocky Mountains, including Pikes Peak near Colorado Springs; and to Florida to visit our daughter Dana and her husband Frank.

Another trip to Estes Park, Colorado, this time in 1976, turned out to be quite a hair-raising adventure, because we had a brush with disaster and narrowly escaped getting caught up in the Big Thompson Canyon Flood of July 31, 1976. This flood turned out to be the deadliest flash flood in Colorado's recorded history. The flash flood was caused by a thunderstorm stalling over the upper part of the Big Thompson River. A total of between 12 and 14 inches of rain fell during a four-hour period in the mountains around the resort town of Estes Park, with nowhere for the water to go except down the steep, narrow walls of the canyon. The flash flooding killed 144 people and caused $35 million worth of property damage in 1977 dollar values. Fortunately, our family heeded the warnings and high-tailed it out of the area before tragedy struck.

It would be difficult, as well as exhausting for the reader, to provide a detailed account of all of my many trips, so in the interest of time, I have decided to focus on a few highlights of my travels in order to capture the flavor of some of my more memorable trips. These include: some of my trips with Cargill; two of my major consulting trips; one of our elder hostel trips; and finally, trips involving the military after my retirement, including squadron reunions and the Honor Flight that Von and I took to Washington D.C. in 2012.

Cargill Business Trips

Travel had been a large part of my life at Cargill, and some of my Cargill travels also involved Von, because in the late 1970s and early 1980s, when our salesforce went after the

With Von outside my office at Cargill's Lake Office before a 25 Year Club Dinner. Courtesy of Cargill, Incorporated.

feedlot business as we were instructed to do, we developed a plan to engage both the feedlot owner/operator and his wife. (It so happened in those days that feedlot operators and managers were exclusively male.) We quickly figured out that the wife was a very important part of the management of the feedlot, because in many cases, she had a great deal of influence over her husband. Consequently, on special occasions, our salesforce designed seminars where we would bring in select groups of feedlot operators and their wives and pay their lodging expenses. The feedlot operator would be attending business sessions that our salesforce was conducting to introduce new programs for effectively raising livestock, usually involving the nutrition and health care of cattle, how to bring in new cattle, and so forth.

During these same business seminars, the salesforce also provided programs for the wives, so while the husbands were attending the livestock sessions, the wives would often be attending a luncheon or dinner theater production. In our keynote sessions, we tried to line up various forms of entertainment and programs, such as motivational speakers or humorists, that would appeal to both the feedlot managers and their wives. Cargill was very supportive of having the wives of the salesforce become part of our marketing strategy. The wives of the salesforce reps would meet the wives of our prospects

Chapter Five: Travel Memoirs

(Top) Von and I boarding the Cargill plane on the way to a seminar. *(Bottom)* Our Cargill office in the air. Courtesy of Cargill, Incorporated.

Getting It Right

With Von at the Grand Island, Nebraska Feed Lot Seminar in 1984. Courtesy of Cargill, Incorporated.

and customers, engaging and connecting with them and helping to create an atmosphere of "one big family."

Over time, Von became a great emissary for Cargill, and Cargill was all for having Von travel to various seminars and meet the feedlot operators and their wives and help with registering them for the seminar. She interacted very well with the other ladies, helping to guide them through activities and enjoying entertaining programs with them.

Von would not only attend the larger feedlot seminars, but she would also go with me to some of the National Cattlemen's Conventions. At these meetings, the Cargill salesforce would have a display booth, and we would also entertain the feedlot operators and their wives if they attended. Von really enjoyed attending all of these business seminars, because she was meeting new people and making new friends. And people really liked Von, because she had such a winning personality, was fun-loving, and adventurous, and was so easy to get along with. She turned out to be an excellent representative for Cargill.

At the Cargill Feedlot Seminar in Grand Island, Nebraska, in 1984, Von was asked to introduce the dinner theater program for the feedlot operators' wives. Von was not accustomed to public speaking and appeared to be rather nervous. One of the program organizers noticed that Von was uneasy about the prospect of getting up in front of such a large crowd and talking. She tactfully approached Von and offered to help her introduce the program. Of course Von readily agreed to this. When the program organizer left, a lady who was sitting beside Von at the table, leaned over and whispered to her, "I knew you were one of those big wigs when you sat down." Von got a real kick out of this and would tell that story over and over again—about the time that she was a "big wig" at the Cargill Feedlot Seminar!

Cargill Fishing Trips

The Feed Division employees had a great tradition at Cargill of going on an annual fishing trip which served to enhance the informal networking in our salesforce.

Von made a scrapbook of one of these trips for me, and I am including a paraphrased excerpt from it here. According to Von's account as recorded in the scrapbook:

> *While snooping through the attic, I came across many, many stories. One of those stories takes us back to 1965, a busy year in the life of the product manager for—cattle feed—dairy feed—hog feed—horse feed, dog food, and almost any other Nutrena product you'd care to mention. That also included the role of training director. After spending a very hectic fall,*

Chapter Five: Travel Memoirs

With Les Cottrill during our 1965 Cargill fishing trip on Lake Nipigon, Ontario, holding our catch of the day. Courtesy of Cargill, Incorporated.

Frying potatoes with Les Cottrill and washing dishes on our fishing trip. Courtesy of Cargill, Incorporated.

winter, and early spring holding meetings on the road selling the new product, Controlled-Release Liquid Supplement (CLS), it was decided that Jim needed some R & R. All options were considered, and it ended up that the company fishing trip to Lake Nipigon, a large lake in Ontario, was (selected) for dollars per minute of relaxation and won hands down. Jim's was the deciding vote, of course!

One of the highlights of the June fishing trip on Lake Nipigon was a candlelight dinner served aboard the swift Canadian lake fishing boat called, "The Bud," as it moved gracefully from one fishing spot to the next in the dark of night. Two of the more sought after jobs aboard "The Bud," were washing the dishes and cooking the fried potatoes. These prime jobs were shared equally by Jim and his friend who wore a black hat (Les Cottrill). This duo washed and fried and washed and fried, but although everyone was receptive to the sparkling clean dishes, utensils, and pans, no one it seemed, after taking the first bite, was very interested in eating the fried potatoes.

After a prolonged investigation, it was discovered that, during some time spent in rough waters, "The Bud" took in a considerable amount of soapy water which had spilled over into the frying pan as the potatoes were being prepared for the candlelight dinner.

The next morning news of Jim's reassignment was posted on the swift ship "Bud's" bulletin board. The notice read: "No more shall Jim McDougall and his friend in the black hat be allowed to do dishes and cook fried potatoes simultaneously aboard the swift Canadian Lake Cruiser, 'The Bud' . . . Never, Never More!"

Elder Hostels (Road Scholar Trips)

In 1988, shortly after I retired, Von and I got busy looking for travel ideas, and we noticed an ad about the Elder Hostels, which later became known as the Road Scholar Program. This was before the age of search engines such as "Google." We spotted a travel brochure about the Elder Hostels, and we wrote and requested more information. We then received some Elder Hostel travel catalogues in the mail, looked through them and chose an option to learn about wolves in Northern Minnesota. Both Von and I thought that looked very intriguing. So off we went to the International Wolf Center in Ely, in the summer of 1989. This was our first experience in what was to become a series of of very enjoyable and memorable Elder Hostel adventures.

The Wolf Center Elder Hostel was hosted at Vermillion College, which is a two-year community college in Ely,

Minnesota, adjacent to the Boundary Waters Canoe Area. Since it was summertime, the student housing wasn't being used, so Von and I and most of the other Elder Hostel attendees, stayed in the Vermillion College dorms.

From the time I first discovered them, I've always been intrigued with the concept of the Elder Hostel. The way the Elder Hostel works is that some enterprising individual contacts a particular college representative and says, "I'd like to rent part of your college for a week, and I'd like to use the dining and lodging facilities." The Elder Hostel organizer and the college representative agree on a price, and then the cost is divided up among all the attendees, and that becomes the housing cost for the week. In the case of our Elder Hostel in Ely, we worked with a woman I'll call Mrs. Jones. Mrs. Jones looked into everything you would want to know about wolves, and then she lined up speakers, guides, field trips etc. At the Wolf Center Elder Hostel, Von and I boarded a bus with Mrs. Jones and the other participants and explored a wolf's den, examined the carcass of a deer killed by a pack of wolves, and learned how to howl back and forth to the wolves in the dark of night.

Listening to the wolves howl at the Ely Wolf Center was quite a remarkable experience for Von and me. We learned that when wolves howl, the wolves in other packs will tend to answer. They howl back and forth. That's what we were listening for during one of our nocturnal field

Chapter Five: Travel Memoirs

Our group at the Wolf Center Elder Hostel in Ely, Minnesota, in 1989, with all the poor trusting souls on our infamous bog walk *(bottom)*. Von is bringing up the rear.

trips. We were all encouraged to howl back at the wolves during our field trip. I figured that I had a head start on the other participants in howling like a wolf, because I had been practicing on my own just for fun for years.

During our nocturnal "wolf howling" field trip, the other participants were all sitting in the bus without making a sound, listening intently, and waiting with baited breath for the wolves to start howling. The bus had its lights turned off, and we were all just sitting there in the total darkness. Von and I happened to be sitting by the front door of the bus, and I whispered to Von, "Wait here—I'm going to try something." I snuck out of the bus unnoticed (except by Von), and the people in the bus started trying to call the wolves. I secretly stationed myself about a half a block away, and suddenly unleashed my best wolf impression. I must have been pretty convincing, because Von told me that the people in the bus thought those ferocious wolves were howling back at them and sounded so close that they were practically biting the tires!

Of course, Von wasn't scared, and I think before long, everyone became rather suspicious about that. I had a lot of fun with that particular prank. I figure in this life, it pays to have a sense of humor and to never miss out on a prime opportunity to have a little fun.

The "bog walk" at the Wolf Center the next day was quite an experience! The lady who was assigned to lead the bog walk was supposed to venture out the day before the hike and check out the route and the conditions of the bog. It became increasingly clear as our group of hikers slogged along through the bog, that our guide had not done her homework. We quickly figured out that our fearless leader didn't know what the heck she was doing or where she was taking us that day.

With Von at the Cargill Retirees' Christmas Dinner in Chippewa Falls, Wisconsin, 2012. Courtesy of Cargill, Incorporated.

I vividly recall our hiking group wandering further and further into the bog, and how we kept going on and on following our leader in blind faith. Before long, we all realized that the wet moss in the bog was getting deeper and deeper, and our feet were getting wetter and wetter. I remember becoming kind of concerned that this lady didn't know what she was doing or where she was going. I thought to myself, "She might even lead us off of a cliff into deep water, for all we know!" Anyway, Von and I certainly didn't want to end up swimming around in the bog. One gentleman and I were talking back and forth and pretty soon a small plane appeared in the sky overhead, and the fellow started waving his arms wildly and shouting, "Help, down here—we don't know where we are!" The plane was up pretty high and of course, the pilot couldn't hear us. Then the guy started waving his arms even more frantically and yelling, "We're serious—we need rescuing down here!"

Fortunately, our leader eventually got us turned around, because we clearly didn't know where we were going. It probably amounted to about two hours that we were trudging through the bog getting soggier and soggier, but it seemed like a lot longer than two hours at the time! We were very relieved once we found our way out of the bog and changed into dry clothes.

Some of our expeditions as retirees were closer to home of course. Von and I also became involved in Cargill Cares, a group of Cargill retirees, after I retired. We would attend informational seminars, go on field trips, and participate in service projects, such as packing food bags for the Feed My Starving Children Program and ringing the Salvation Army Bell at Christmastime.

"Cargill businesses and facilities and their employees also give through more than 350 employee-led Cargill Cares Councils worldwide. The councils provide support for local charitable and civic organizations and programs such as food relief agencies, school and youth programs, and local environmental projects."*

Consulting Trips

CONSULTING TRIP TO SPAIN (PRE-RETIREMENT)
In the summer of 1968, I took a trip to Europe representing Cargill to consult with the Hens Feed Company. I visited several countries while on this trip, including: Belgium, the Netherlands, Spain, Portugal, France, and Germany.

The original purpose of the trip was to explore the potential for a complete beef feed program for Hens, which focused on how to handle the proportion of roughage in the feed. Hens was headquartered in Antwerp, Belgium, and they also

---
*— www.Cargill.com

Two of the Hens Reps in Brussels, Belgium, 1968. Courtesy of Cargill, Incorporated.

had a strong presence in Spain. Since I was over in Belgium consulting with Hens, I was also asked to do some consulting for them regarding their business interests in Spain.

On this particular consulting trip with Hens, my hosts and I started out in Antwerp, Belgium. Coincidentally, my daughter, Betsy, who was aged 16 at the time, was traveling to France with a French language study group, and her plane landed in Brussels while I was in the city. My host, Jan Jans, a Hens sales employee and his daughter, Frieda, (who was Betsy's pen pal for her French studies), took me to the airport to meet Betsy's plane for a very brief visit. (Betsy informed me recently that Frieda, who spoke seven languages, grew up to be an international interpreter.) During the time I was staying in Belgium, my hosts from Hens and I made a brief sightseeing trip to the Netherlands. I have some pictures of the windmills and the canals along with the Dutch countryside. I flew with some Hens sales reps from Belgium to Barcelona, and from there I proceeded to do some additional consulting work in Spain and Portugal.

While I was consulting in Spain, I was asked about some problems occurring with the "Brave Bulls," which is how the Spanish people refer to the ferocious bulls that are raised for bull fighting. The breeders who raised these fighting bulls were quite concerned about how aggressive the bulls were becoming. The fighting bulls' ability to inflict harm was getting to the point where it was more and more dangerous, and I suspected that the breeders were also worried about public opinion. I think the breeders wanted these bulls to be big and ferocious-looking but not extremely aggressive. They thought maybe a large feed company, such as Hens, with a presence in Spain, would know something about feeding programs that would help them achieve their objectives with the bulls.

Consulting in Spain in 1968. Courtesy of Cargill, Incorporated.

Chapter Five: Travel Memoirs

(Top) Consulting with beef farmers in Spain. *(Bottom)* The Brave Bulls I was consulting about in Spain. Courtesy of Cargill, Incorporated.

So it happened that Hens was consulted about nutrition regarding the Brave Bulls, and Hens in turn consulted with Cargill. Since I was going to be over in Europe anyway on some other business deals, I was assigned the task of representing Cargill to Hens.

When I arrived in Spain, the Hens reps and I drove through the Andalusian countryside along the southern coast to visit bull farms where the beef producers raised the Brave Bulls. Most of these people could not speak English very well. What they would do is gather up all their bullfighting paraphernalia when they knew we were coming and lay it on the grass by their house. Then we were supposed to "ooh and aah" and make a big fuss about the various pieces of equipment and wardrobe items they had to fight the bulls with.

Then I would go out and survey the beef producer's herd, where he was raising the Brave Bulls. In these herds, there would be younger bulls being raised for bull fights. The Hens reps and I would ask about how the farmers bred these bulls and how they fed them. There were some interesting things going on. After carefully surveying the situation, it looked to me to be a fairly simple fix. Many of these Spanish beef producers didn't fully understand how to introduce feed to cattle or how to keep them properly fed at the various stages of growth. They also weren't fully aware of what made the animals sick, how to treat illnesses, or how to keep the animal healthy in the first place.

What I ended up suggesting was that the Spanish beef producer should feed the bull more energy, (that is, more carbs and less protein) and let him develop a little fat so he would look bigger. The bull would retain a lot of his ferociousness of course, and he would be a bigger, meaner looking animal—without necessarily actually being meaner and more aggressive. The translator would carry on this conversation in Spanish with the feeders that I didn't understand. The essence of it was that the producers were going to feed the bull more energy. And they were going to be careful about how they did it so they didn't get too much feed too quickly into the bull when he wasn't used to it.

The Hens sales reps then took me around and showed me the places where the beef producers kept the younger bulls, as well as the special trucks they had to transport these smaller, younger bulls to the church festivals where there were smaller bull rings set up. I learned that some of the teenaged boys were supposed to go out and fight these young bulls for practice, however, I didn't witness any of these practice bull fights while I was on my consulting trip. Special trucks had been built that could haul six or seven young bulls at the same time. There were compartments built into the truck that separated the bulls, confining them in close quarters and preventing them from moving around too much. I was impressed with those trucks because they were a foreign concept to me, having been designed with a unique purpose in mind.

The Hens reps also took me to Portugal where men fight the bulls on horseback. I distinctly remember meeting one particular individual who had been fighting bulls on horseback. This man had four wristwatches on his arm. I asked him why, but because of the language barrier, I couldn't understand his explanation. Nobody I was with could figure out exactly why he was wearing all those wristwatches, but my hunch was that he was trying to keep track of different time zones in contacting customers that he shipped bulls to internationally.

That consulting trip to Spain was quite interesting. I didn't know a thing about bull fighting when I started, but I learned quite a lot about it during my visit. I did attend a bullfight while I was on the trip and saw one of the bullfighters get thrown up into the air about 10 feet and then get carried out on a stretcher. I never found out if he made it or not. Tourists don't typically find out those things. But these bulls—they mean business. They want to kill you! The bullfighters on horses throw darts called banderillo's into the bulls' backs, and it makes them madder than hornets. The crowd cheers wildly if they think the matador made a good, clean kill after a ferocious fight. Also, they

Chapter Five: Travel Memoirs

throw their hats and flowers into the ring and display all kinds of theatrics when they think that the matador does an outstanding job.

I saw the bull fight in de Palma de Mallorca (Majorca). This is one of the islands that stretches out in the western Mediterranean to the east of Spain. We flew there from Madrid.

As we were getting ready to take off in a plane to fly to Majorca, I'll never forget when one of the passengers on the plane—I think he was a salesman with Hens—shouted: "All right everybody, take out your passports and put 'em between your teeth, because it will be easier to identify the bodies!" You can imagine the reaction of the other passengers! That crazy guy—I'll never forget that! It just goes to show you how some people have a very strange sense of humor.

The Spanish Civil War had been raging on just before WWII and turned out to be a very bitter struggle. General Franco was one of the rebels and a key leader. (Coincidentally, I saw Franco, in person, walking through the airport terminal in Madrid during my consulting trip to Spain.) I wanted to see where these battles had been fought. As we drove along on my consulting jobs from Barcelona to Seville, the Hens reps pointed out these battlefields to me. I also remember meeting up with Jim North in Seville. Jim was Cargill's Director of the Feed Division at that time.

Jim left that area and flew home shortly after that. He called Von when he got home and said, "I suppose you're wondering about Jim. The last time I saw him, he had a Spaniard on each side of him talking to him like mad, and I don't think Jim understood a word either of them said." Von got a real kick out of that.

I made some interesting observations about the Spanish work ethic on this consulting trip. From my American vantage point, the Spaniards had unconventional work hours. At this time in Spain, most people worked very close to where they lived. They generally didn't arrive at work until late in the morning. They ate in the middle of the afternoon and then afterward they often rested or took a siesta. If they returned to work after that, they weren't usually done until about 8 or 9 o'clock in the evening because they didn't typically work in the morning. If they had visitors like me, they took them to a bar or restaurant when they went to lunch. They expected you to sample some of that particular establishment's best wine.

If you were invited out to dinner in the evening, your Spanish hosts would accompany you to a popular bar or restaurant, and they brought a wine skin out. They put wine in a container that resembled a leather pouch, called a Bota Bag, and it had a little nozzle in it. I saw the Spaniards do tricky things with it. For example, they would squeeze the wine skin and aim the stream of wine on their

Chapter Five: Travel Memoirs

(Top) With my parents, Edith and Chester (Chet) in Germany in 1968. *(Bottom)* On a boat trip down the Rhine with my parents and my sister, Edyie, and her husband, Gene (taking the picture).

forehead, and it would run down the side of their nose and into their mouth. The guys I observed performing this maneuver seemed to think this was a pretty impressive skill. The traditional wine skin is called a zahato.

> *The zahato is the traditional goatskin bottle of the Basque shepherds. With its narrow nozzle, it is possible to drink "zurrust," i.e., intercepting the jet without touching the bottle.**

My hosts and their friends were performing all kinds of tricks trying to outdo each other "Drinking Zurrust" for the benefit of their guests. I just watched and wisely didn't enter the competition.

When it comes to drinking wine, these Spaniards were masters! At the meals I attended, they ordered several different kinds of wine, and they probably put the wine on an expense account. By the time most people got done drinking wine, they weren't always sure whether they had eaten or not!

After I finished my consulting work in Spain, I flew to Paris and stayed overnight. From Paris, I went over to see my father and mother, who were visiting my sister, Edythe (Eydie), and her husband, Gene. Gene was an army

---

*— wikipedia.org

doctor at the time and was stationed at a military base near Frankfurt, Germany. I stayed overnight at Eydie and Gene's place, and then the five of us (Eydie and Gene, my parents, and I) all went on a very enjoyable and memorable cruise down the Rhine River together.

CONSULTING TRIP TO UKRAINE AND POLAND (POST RETIREMENT)

In 1992, as Von and I were settling into the routine of retired life, I was contacted by Ralph Grier about a rather interesting opportunity. Ralph, who had retired from Cargill about the same time I did, had been involved in training and many other tasks with the Feed Division. In fact, he was manager for one of Cargill's Chinese operations in Taiwan. Somehow or other, Ralph got in contact with a government organization called VOCA (Volunteers for Overseas Cooperative Assistance), which is operated through Agricultural Cooperative Development International (ACDI).

Ralph had been contacted by VOCA with a request to do some consulting in Ukraine. Ukraine became an independent country again when the Soviet Union dissolved in 1991. The people of Ukraine had lived under Communist rule for decades, and now that they were free agents, there were a number of businessmen, farmers, and other individuals who wanted to explore how they could learn from successful American enterprises. There were many projects that the Ukrainians wanted to get involved with in the free enterprise system, but they needed help and advice. So the plan was that various consultants from the United States would travel to Ukraine to offer their expertise and assist the population in getting started with various businesses and other endeavors.

What VOCA wanted Ralph to do was to train farmers in Ukraine how to raise hogs more efficiently. I don't believe that Ralph was familiar enough with the hog business to want to embark on this particular consulting trip, so he approached me to see if I'd be interested. One day, when I was working in my front lawn, Ralph stopped by and asked me if I'd consider accepting VOCA's assignment, which he explained in detail to me. I told him that I wasn't interested, because I didn't want to be away from my family that long.

Ralph left, but I heard back from him shortly after that. He said, "I'd like to talk to you about your concern involving being away from your family." Once again, I told him that Von and I were enjoying retired life together, and that I didn't want us to be apart for that length of time. Ralph then replied, "Well, VOCA would be willing to send both you and your wife over." This time, I indicated a willingness to take VOCA up on the opportunity, in large part because of Von's love of travel and desire to have new adventures. Shortly afterward, VOCA started corresponding with me to set up the trip.

Von and I traveled to Washington, DC, on November 4th, 1992, to prepare for our trip to Ukraine. Prior to our departure, Von and I met with some government VOCA officials to find out more about what was involved in my assignment. While we were in Washington D.C., Von and I had dinner with my cousin, General Jack Nicholson, and his lovely wife, Sophie, at the Quality Hotel on Capitol Hill. General Jack did a nice job of explaining the United States' relationship with the Ukraine, since he had considerable experiences in the military with international affairs, and this proved to be very helpful to Von and me.

Von and I flew from Washington to Kyiv on November 5th, 1992. In Kyiv we were met by an interpreter and by the U.S. government representative who was responsible for some of the VOCA operations, including in Ukraine. I recall that on the first night after we arrived, the U.S. government representative took Von and me on a brief tour of Kyiv and then to a nice restaurant in the Hotel Kreshchatik the first night. There were about ten of us in the group. We were seated, and when the waiter took our order, since none of the people in our group spoke Ukrainian, we had to have the menu read and translated for us. Von and I both ordered a dish we thought we'd probably enjoy, as did the other people at our table. A short time later, as

Sightseeing with Von in Lubny, Ukraine. 1991.

the waiter brought our food out to us, he seemed to have no trouble at all remembering who ordered what. As he was placing our dinners in front of us, we noticed that all the dishes looked exactly the same, even though we had all placed different orders. As I recall, the dinner we were served was Chicken Kyiv, which at least seemed appropriate, given where we were. But it was really perplexing that the waiter would spend so much time going through the motions of carefully writing down our various orders and then bring out the very same dish to all of us. We suspected that either he didn't understand our orders, couldn't keep track of who ordered what, or that was all that the restaurant had available. We all got a real kick out of that incident.

The Hotel Kreshchatik was very nice, but Von and I weren't sure whether we should drink the tap water or not. So when we were getting ready for bed and we wanted to brush our teeth, I went down to the front desk to request some clean drinking water. The receptionist gave me a bottle, and I went back upstairs to our room and discovered that it contained white wine! The guy at the front desk must not have understood me, because I had distinctly asked for drinking water. I think his English was about as good as my Ukrainian.

Right off the bat, we met our driver and interpreter, who were assigned to us during our stay. The driver drove us with the interpreter to the town of Lubny, located in north-central Ukraine, where we would be staying while I did my consulting work. When we arrived in Lubny, Von and I were introduced to a very nice lady named Luda, who managed the computer factory in Lubny and was taking some time off to host Von and me in her home during our stay. Her husband, Lionia (Lona), was the doctor assigned to the computer factory. It was apparent that the way the

Our hosts, Luda and Lona (center), and their house in Lubny, Ukraine.

Chapter Five: Travel Memoirs

With Von and Luda in her living room.

health program was administered in Ukraine was through a common work place, and my impression was that Lona basically made up the factory's entire health operation. Von and I got the impression that Luda and Lona had previously been pretty high up in the Communist party.

Lona would usually come home from working as a doctor in the factory at about 3:00 in the afternoon. He and Luda owned a television set, which was considered quite a luxury. Lona would ask Von to join him in the living room where the TV was located, and they would watch some sort of soap opera or telenovela entirely in Spanish. I thought to myself, "Here are two people, one who speaks only Ukrainian and one who speaks only English, and they're both watching a program all in Spanish." That really baffled me, but Von seemed fine with the idea.

During this consulting trip to Ukraine, which primarily focused on improving hog production, I would travel almost every day to visit farms, feed mills, factories, or some other agricultural facility, and Von would stay back with Luda. Von and Luda learned to communicate quite well together and seemed to really enjoy each other's company. They would cook up a storm, and Luda taught Von to make dishes like borscht and Ukrainian breads and desserts. On many days Luda and Von would prepare a big dinner and then Luda and Lona would invite different people to come over for dinner and meet us. There was a frequent guest named Petrov, whom we believed was a physical therapist or a chiropractor. He would give me massages, and they felt great.

The Ukrainians would typically serve a lot of vodka. It seemed that everybody had to have vodka at social gatherings. Neither Von nor I had ever drunk much vodka, so we didn't indulge much in this custom.

Something I found very interesting was that after dinner, most of the men excused themselves and went upstairs to a room where they smoked. I didn't really feel like spending much time in a smoke-filled room, but I did go up there once, and once was enough for me. It was very difficult to have a conversation when you were trying not to choke on the smoke.

Most days I would go out with my driver and interpreter to various hog farms. On one particular farm, the farmer had two sows, and one of the sows had just had piglets. I soon discovered that a farm with just a few hogs, such as between two and five, was considered a relatively large hog operation in Ukraine. I was rather bewildered, because the farmer only had two hogs! I attempted to talk to the farmer about how he could become a larger operation, which was a bit of an uphill battle, working through an interpreter.

Another one of my primary tasks during this consulting trip was to give advice to young men being discharged from the Ukrainian military on how to establish

Consulting with farmers out in the field in Ukraine.

themselves in farming. The Ukrainian government plan was based loosely on our homestead plan in the United States. The Ukrainian government would assign a person so many hectares of land, say around 40, and then he had four years to make this land productive by producing animals or crops for sale. Most of the young people I worked with had been enlisted in the Ukrainian military and had served on the Chinese-Russian border. In talking with one young man, I discovered he was quite impressed that he had been given some land that he could own, and as far as being productive was concerned, this wasn't foremost in his mind. He asked me, "What will happen in four years if the land isn't productive?" I replied, "Well, the government will take it back." And the young man said, "They will never take it back," and then made a gesture like he was shooting a gun. It appeared that maybe he really meant it.

I traveled around to different collective farms during our visit to Ukraine. The huge problem they had was that these big collective farms had operational machinery, but the machinery mainly consisted of very large items of equipment that were designed to farm large tracts of land—and here were these farmers with their 40 hectares of land and no smaller types of machinery suited for smaller tracks of land. At that time in Ukraine, there was no place to buy any machinery. That was a very serious problem. My thought was if there was some way that the United States could provide the Ukrainian independent farmers with machinery that would fit the size of their smaller farms, maybe the Ukrainian farmers could borrow the machinery on loan. Of course, this idea wasn't practical, given the obvious problems with logistics.

The challenging situation I discovered in Ukraine was that the small independent farmers would have to go and beg the collective farms to lend them the machinery. This arrangement was unlikely to happen, as the larger, collective farmers would understandably consider the smaller, independent farmers to be direct competitors, and the large collectives had little incentive to help out the smaller independents.

This turned out to be a pretty frustrating situation, especially because of the political problems the Ukrainians faced. I knew the kind of machinery the farmers needed, but I wasn't encouraged about their prospects, based on what I was observing.

While visiting the collective farms, I noticed something that I found to be pretty remarkable. The noon meal was the main meal of the day. It was a heavy meal and always seemed to be served with vodka. After the meal was finished, most of the people disappeared, and I realized that they were off taking naps. I was dumbfounded by this. Here they're supposed to be farming, and they're taking a siesta in the middle of the day! This was quite a contrast to the way American farms were being run and simply didn't make sense to me.

I did quite a bit of sightseeing while I traveled from site to site during my consulting work. Von and I spent most of our time in central Ukraine, and I had expressed an interest in seeing some of the battlefields from WWII where the Russian and German tanks fought. My hosts did try to show me some of these battlefields, but since the war had happened so long ago, they were either unaware of, or didn't remember, many details.

One of the more interesting excursions Von and I embarked on while in Ukraine involved visiting the department stores as well as the market, to witness how the wheels of

Chapter Five: Travel Memoirs

Von browsing in a department store in Lubny, Ukraine.

Von all dressed up Ukrainian style.

Chapter Five: Travel Memoirs

Shopping for car parts in the Lubny marketplace.

commerce were operating in a country that had been under Communist control up until about a year before our visit.

While in the department store, Von and I saw racks of clothing items, for instance, dresses, which were all virtually the same color and style but came in different sizes. We noticed that the clothing seemed to be of poor quality, as well as being overpriced. Next, we walked over to the toy section and saw much of the same situation. The tricycles and bicycles looked like they were just junk. We were not impressed. As we left the department store, Von and I wondered if anyone ever actually shopped there, as the aisles seemed empty except for the sales clerks.

While we were staying in their home, our hosts, Luda and Lona, wanted Von to try on one of their huge fur hats, which Ukraine is known for. Von tried one on, but I didn't think it was a very flattering look for her. She looked like she was all hat and no body. Luda and Lona, to the contrary, exclaimed about how wonderful Von looked in the hat and insisted that we go to the local market to buy a hat for Von to take home. They gave us directions that next Saturday, and Von and I gave in and trekked off to experience the market.

Once Von and I arrived at the market, we felt that it was somewhat like going to the Minnesota State Fair back home. There were many trucks backing up and unloading all sorts of goods. There were all kinds of produce, meat, clothing, souvenirs, etc.—quite a menagerie of merchandise. I had asked my hosts, "What if I had a car that broke down and I needed a part?" I was told, "You just have to go to the market and find another broken down car like yours and find a part that fits your car." Well that didn't seem like a very practical system to me—to have to scrounge around and find a similar car to yours that was broken down and could be harvested for parts.

I could see quite a few disadvantages with this system of having to go and try your luck at the market, but this seemed to be where people in Ukraine actually acquired what they needed. My impression was that their market became a bartering system, where people argued about the prices. My dad, who loved bartering, would have been in his glory at this market.

Von and I eventually found the fur hat vendors at the market, but we didn't end up buying a hat, because it would have taken up most of the space in Von's suitcase! Von did buy some nesting dolls in Kyiv before leaving for Poland. She had found a set of dolls she wanted in the Hotel Kreshchatik's souvenir shop in Kyiv, but the sales clerks didn't know how much to charge in U.S. dollars. They asked Von how much she thought the dolls were worth, and Von said she didn't know. Eventually, a price was agreed upon, and Von ended up with a set of nesting dolls which we have kept to this day.

About two weeks into the trip, representatives from VOCA decided that I had done about as much as I could to help in terms of consulting in Ukraine, and they asked me if I would be willing to spend the rest of my time on the trip abroad helping with a request from the Polish government to provide suggestions regarding feed milling. I agreed to accommodate this request, as Von seemed in favor of it, so we prepared to leave Kyiv, Ukraine, and head for Warsaw, Poland, on November 19th.

When it was time to say goodbye to our hosts, Luda and Lona, I decided to pay them well. Although consulting through VOCA is done on a volunteer basis, Von and

I had been given a large sum of cash (around $5,000) to cover our expenses. I didn't really like the idea of being in a foreign country and being responsible for such a large amount of money. The Hotel Kreshchatik was very expensive, I thought. The bill was for over $100 for a room for the night. I ended up paying my hosts, Luda and Lona, that amount per night for our stay. They seemed delighted about that.

Von and I encountered a bit of a problem with the language barrier as we tried to leave Ukraine for Poland. We naively assumed that flying out of Ukraine would be just like it was in America at that time, where you went up to the gate and showed your ticket and then got on board. Not so in Ukraine! The government officials evidently had to do a lot of checking on you before they let you board an airplane. Even though Von and I arrived at the airport well ahead of time to make sure we caught our flight, for a while we didn't think the officials were going to let us get on the plane! They had a very abrupt and suspicious manner, and seemed to be going through a lot of checking to clear us. I suppose they were also checking to make sure we paid our hotel bills, etc. Finally right before the plane was scheduled to take off, the officials told us, "Okay, you're cleared to go. You can fly." So Von and I got on the plane and took off. We were quite relieved to finally depart from the airport, as we were starting to get a little worried.

In Warsaw, Von and I stayed in lodgings that resembled our American motels. The place we stayed was called the MotorRest Hotel. It also had a restaurant where we ate some of our meals. I wasn't too comfortable leaving Von alone at our lodgings while I went on my consulting trips in Poland, but she seemed to get along all right.

Right off the bat in Poland, Von ran into a minor cultural snafu. The restaurant at the motel did not have handles on their cups. Von apparently had never had to drink her coffee out of a "handle-less" cup. She kept asking for a cup with a handle, and finally the waiter exclaimed, "Oh an ear! You want a cup with an ear!" The Polish people apparently use the term "ear" instead of handle when referring to cups. So from then on we requested cups with "ears."

As far as my consulting trip to Poland, I was again assigned a driver and an interpreter, and there were usually a couple of other individuals who rode along with us in the car. As in Ukraine, we would drive around to different places out in the country, such as farms, feed mills and factories. The farmers in Poland seemed to be experiencing similar problems to those I had learned about in Ukraine as far as lack of equipment and machinery etc., but the problems weren't quite as severe. The Polish people's prospects for progress seemed somewhat more favorable. Whereas in Ukraine I concentrated on hog production, the Polish farmers were more interested in the milling aspects of grain production. The Polish farmers I consulted with tended to represent the larger, more prosperous farming operations that were somewhat similar to farms in the United States, but were not nearly as productive.

In the U.S. at that time, we had developed a grind and mix operation mounted on a truck. This would usually involve a worker who had a machine, who could go in and grind a particular type of grain, such as barley, and mix it into the feed. This was a service the worker would hire himself out to perform, and he would provide the service to multiple farms. His job was to grind and mix feed for the livestock. This was a service that I thought would be a really good fit for the Polish farmers. However, this requires salesmanship. In other words, someone has to go out and explain the service to the farmer and get him to agree to the purchase and arrange how he was going to pay for it. These basic marketing concepts were totally foreign to the Polish farmers. They were unfamiliar with the capitalist system. Even though the Polish farmers were much further along in terms of making progress in agriculture than those in Ukraine, I still had considerable difficulty explaining the concepts of free enterprise to them.

As a general rule, I found the Polish people to be less affable and friendly than the Ukrainian people. They seemed more stern and serious with less of a sense of humor. They tended to be more skeptical and to ask more questions and to grill me more on the details. They also seemed more interested in learning English than the Ukrainians. They seemed to understand what I was talking about and suggesting, but to line up a machine that they'd never seen and to get access to one was quite a stretch for them. I could see the possibility of getting a representative from an implement company over to Poland and lining this up. Theoretically, he would be there to explain everything and make the arrangements to purchase the equipment, but I realized that there would still be huge challenges in order for the kind of substantial agricultural progress that I envisioned could potentially happen in Poland.

A lot of the people we were visiting in Poland were not just common workers but were leaders. These leaders would invite someone in whom they were trying to impress and would sit them down at a table with an interpreter. Pretty soon an alcoholic beverage would appear. The visitor got the sense that the host had been saving this special bottle for quite a while. The host wanted his guest to taste the bottle from his stash that he'd saved for special visitors. Apparently, the way the Polish people impressed others at that time was to give them a sample of their very best liquor.

Von and I were scheduled to fly back home out of Warsaw to the U.S. on December 3rd, 1992. On our last night in

Warsaw, Von and I were instructed by our VOCA representatives to find a very nice restaurant of our choice and treat ourselves to a special meal. Von and I walked around downtown Warsaw and found a restaurant that looked inviting.

Once we were seated at our table and given menus, we were surprised that more customers weren't present in what appeared to be such a nice establishment. We didn't have an interpreter but managed to communicate the menu selections for our dinner orders. Then the waiter motioned for Von and me to follow him and go over to a wall stacked with wine bottles containing all different kinds of wine. The waiter conveyed to us that now that we had ordered, it was time for us to choose a bottle of wine to go with our meal.

Von and I spent a considerable amount of time selecting the wine. We finally picked out a bottle that appealed to us and returned to our table. When the waiter came back over, he had a white napkin folded over his arm, and he proceeded to pop the cork on the wine bottle. The waiter poured a little of the wine in my glass and motioned for me to taste it. A diabolical thought entered into my mind, and I wondered what the waiter would do if I didn't like it.

Immediately after I tasted the wine, I grabbed my throat and started choking dramatically like I was in distress. The waiter jumped backwards, and his eyes got as big as saucers. He must have thought that I had been poisoned and that perhaps he had just caused an international incident. I laughed and quickly reassured him that the wine was fine. His face just lit up. Then he knew I was playing a prank and that he'd been had. Von and I got along with him really well after that. When we left, the waiter even gave us a monogrammed plate from the restaurant, which we still have. I remember Von and I often chuckled about that particular incident afterward.

All in all, Von and I looked back on our trip to Ukraine and Poland as memorable, educational, and enjoyable. I believe that the concept behind VOCA was sound, but it was a little ahead of its time. I like to think that I planted some seeds and got the farmers I consulted with thinking about the possibilities of enlarging and improving their livestock and milling operations both in Ukraine and Poland.

Squadron Reunions and Honor Flight

Another aspect of our travels that I'd like to mention, related to the military, were the trips Von and I took together to participate in my naval squadron reunions. In the late 1980s, shortly after I retired from Cargill, my WWII Squadron VPB-52 started getting together periodically. We met annually for a period of about 15 years in a number of cities including: Orlando, Atlanta, Williamsburg,

New Orleans, Houston, Denver, Phoenix, Albuquerque, and San Diego. Von and I really enjoyed attending these reunions, which usually featured activities such as listening to speakers and tours of military installations and military museums, as well as visits to local tourist attractions. Unfortunately, we had to stop getting together when the squadron started getting older, and the logistics of travel became too difficult for many of the members.

One of the last trips Von and I took together was our Honor Flight, which took place on October 6, 2012, through the Twin Cities Honor Flight Network. An Honor Flight is conducted by non-profit organizations dedicated to transporting (by plane) as many United States Military Veterans as possible to Washington D.C., to see the memorials of the respective wars at no cost to the veterans. I was one of the few veterans able to go with their wives, because Von was also a veteran, having served as one of the Navy's WAVES (Women Accepted for Volunteer Emergency Service). Her position was Storekeeper Disbursing Second Class in the Navy from 1944 to 1945. Being able to go on the flight together was an added incentive for Von and me to attend the Honor Flight. Quite a few people had encouraged Von and me to apply to go on an Honor Flight, and we were very happy that we did.

Von and I got up very early in the morning the day of the trip to make the Honor Flight out of the Minneapolis/

With Von on our Honor Flight in 2012.

St. Paul International Airport. We had to be there by 4:30 am. It was a very long day, both because of all the flying time and because there were so many activities packed into a very short time frame. We flew to the nation's capital and saw all of the famous war memorials: Washington, Lincoln, WWII, Korean, Iwo Jima, and Vietnam. Von and I were aware that we would be seeing the war memorials, but we weren't expecting all of the elaborate behind-the-scenes preparation and fanfare that went with the trip.

We were pleasantly surprised by a "mail call" during the outgoing flight, where we received letters and well-wishes regarding our trip from many of our friends and relatives.

The envelopes were the same type and size used for airmail during WWII. Our entire group also received a standing ovation as we departed from the plane on our return flight.

Von and I were very impressed with how well-organized the entire operation turned out to be. As someone who has run many meetings in my professional life, I recognize all the hard work that goes into orchestrating such a massive undertaking.

Conclusion

In closing, I would like to say that I feel very fortunate to have had the opportunity to travel so much in my life. I especially appreciated the trips with my dear wife, Von. She was the best traveling companion anyone could ever hope for. The wish that Von and I always shared was that our children, grandchildren, and great grandchildren would also be able to travel far and wide around our great country and experience some of the many wonders of the world in their lifetimes.

About the Author

James Robert (Jim) McDougall was born in 1923 and grew up on a farm on the outskirts of Le Mars, Iowa. He, along with many from the Greatest Generation, went on to enlist in the United States Navy to fight for his country in WWII. He served as a combat air crewman and bombardier for the 7th Fleet's Black Cat Squadron VPB-52 in the Southwest Pacific from 1943–44. Upon discharge from the Navy in 1946, Jim married the love of his life, Yvonne Welch. The two started college life together, taking full advantage of the GI Bill. Jim earned a B.A. Degree in Biology with a Minor in Education from Yankton College in South Dakota, and a B.S. degree in Agricultural Education from South Dakota State University in Brookings, S.D. He taught Vocational Agriculture in northwest Iowa at the high school level for four years before taking a job with Nutrena, Cargill Inc.'s Animal Feed Division in Minneapolis, Minnesota,

About the Author

The author in Oban, Scotland, standing in front of the McDougall castle.

in 1955. He worked for Cargill in a variety of capacities, including Beef Feed Products Manager, Northern Regional Sales Manager, and Beef Feedlot Nutrition Consultant for Caprock Industries, until his retirement in 1988. Jim and Von enjoyed 68 years of marriage and raised six children— five daughters and one son. Jim and Von traveled to most states in the U.S. and visited many other countries throughout the world, including Ukraine, where Jim consulted in order to help that country expand its free market agricultural industry shortly after the fall of the Soviet Union in 1991.

Jim enjoyed sharing his life stories and because of his background in naval aerial combat in WWII, he was a

About the Author

The author signing books.

sought-after speaker at many military and aviation events, including Wings of the North Air Show, Fort Snelling WWII History Panels, the Minnesota History Museum WWII Panels, and chapters of the Experimental Aircraft

About the Author

Jim as keynote speaker (pictured with Steve Steele) at the Memorial Day Celebration at Purgatory Creek, Eden Prairie, Minnesota, on May 31, 2021.

Association (EAA) and Civil Air Patrol (CAP). In his later years, Jim continued his love of learning and teaching and wanted to leave a lasting legacy for others by writing his memoirs: *Almost Famous*; *Conflict to Combat in the South Pacific*; *The Road to Love: Our Family's Story 1818-1999*; and *Getting it Right: Reflections on a Life Spanning a Century*. Jim found the process of writing his memoirs to be very rewarding and worthwhile and wanted to encourage members of his family and others to share their memoirs as well.

About the Author

Jim lived in Minnetonka, Minnesota, where he was fortunate to remain surrounded by his family as he amassed so many memories of a life well-lived. Sadly, Jim passed away on March 26, 2023, less than two months shy of his 100th birthday. His family decided posthumously that Jim had lived close enough to the 100 mark that they could round up to crediting him with "living a century."

Jim's first memoir was titled *Almost Famous*, because he was "almost" the first baby born in the brand new Sacred Heart Hospital in Le Mars, Iowa, and almost exactly 100 years later, he lived "almost" a century.

This irony would not have been lost on Jim.

www.ingramcontent.com/pod-product-compliance
Lightning Source LLC
Chambersburg PA
CBHW040100070526
44107CB00163B/743